ALL CHARGES DROPPED!

{ VOLUME 1 }

I loved reading, *All Charges Dropped!* Dr Camacho draws on his wealth of Court System experience to share interesting stories that illustrate the good news of Paul's New Testament gospel (justification by faith). A well-written and compelling devotional. A must read for anyone who wants more clarity on what the true gospel means in practical terms.

—Mariellen R. Reiber, Psy.D.

I couldn't stop reading *All Charges Dropped!*, as each story drew me into the courtroom. Written so seamlessly as real-life courtroom verdicts segued into real life biblical truth of God's judgement and forgiveness through Jesus Christ. While reading these stories I gasped, teared up and chuckled at the brilliant writing of Haroldo Camacho. Definitely a five-star book.

—Jan Withers

Against the Law, our works and conscience cannot stand. We are left beaten, broken, and bruised. However, God doesn't just leave us alone in this fallen state. *All Charges Dropped!* emphasizes the grace and comfort of Christ's death on the cross. Haroldo excellently ties in the good news with some interesting and engaging stories. These stories allow for reflection and connection to restoration. Each story brings a different angle, but the same central point. These devotions are great for a daily dose or a necessary recharge of God's word.

—Michael Grundstrom

The stories presented by Mr. Camacho are both real and believable. They are told by a master storyteller with deep insight into the human condition and deep knowledge of the spiritual battles we all face. They are gripping and irresistible to read. They speak of disaster and hope, failure and redemption. But most of all, these stories tell of our deep need and of God's grace and mercy to his children.

—Michael W. Pursley

Haroldo has a unique talent for connecting Scripture to real life situations. His comparisons of human law and justice to God's mercy and grace serve as a reminder of just how blessed we are!

—Carol C. Tucek

All Charges Dropped! is a most inspiring collection of modern-day illustrations of the gospel message. Author Dr. Haroldo Camacho cleverly and eloquently uses heartwarming, courtroom drama as non-fiction parables to convey very real biblical concepts and to illuminate fitting scripture references. The courthouse setting of the narratives is the perfect reminder of the celestial trial in which all humanity stands before the Father, with the Counsellor defending us and the Son being sentenced to death for us that we might be eternally acquitted.

—Rev. Tony Durante
Plantation, Florida

Dr. Camacho in this engaging book recounts what God has done through Jesus the Christ and His Holy Spirit for all humanity through the "real life" stories of court cases he was present for. The forgiveness of our sins and our eternal life with God received by faith in what Jesus the Son of God said and did. Received by each of us by Faith in Jesus. And not by our own Faith but by the Faith we receive from God's Holy Spirit. The stories are varied and touch our hearts in many, many ways. I have recommended this book for all people of all ages.

—Craig Chaddock
Lay Minister, Our Savior Lutheran Church
(Plantation, Florida)

ALL CHARGES DROPPED!

{ VOLUME 1 }

Devotional Narratives from
Earthly Courtrooms to the Throne of Grace

HAROLDO S. CAMACHO

Foreword by Donavon Riley

1517.

*All Charges Dropped! Devotional Narratives from Earthly Courtrooms
to the Throne of Grace, Volume 1*

Published by:
1517 Publishing
PO Box 54032
Irvine, CA 92619-4032

Publisher's Cataloging-In-Publication Data
(Prepared by The Donohue Group, Inc.)

Names: Camacho, Haroldo S., author. | Riley, Donavon, writer of foreword.
Title: All charges dropped! : devotional narratives from Earthly courtrooms
    to the throne of grace.
    Volume 1 / by Haroldo S. Camacho ; foreword by Donavon Riley.
Description: Irvine, CA : 1517 Publishing, [2022] | Also published
    simultaneously in Spanish under title ¡Se retira la demanda! Relatos
    devocionales desde la corte terrenal hasta el trono de la gracia. |
    Includes bibliographical references.
Identifiers: ISBN: 978-1-956658-02-6 (paperback) | 978-1-956658-03-3 (ebook)
Subjects: LCSH: Christianity and law—Prayers and devotions. | Criminal justice,
    Administration of—Religious aspects—Christianity. | Trials—Religious
    aspects—Christianity. | Law (Theology)—Prayers and devotions. |
    God (Christianity)—Mercy. | Christian life. | LCGFT: Devotional literature. |
    BISAC: RELIGION / Christian Living / Devotional. | RELIGION / Christian
    Living / General. | RELIGION / Christian Theology / General.
Classification: LCC: BR115.L28 C36 2022 | DDC: 241.2—dc23

"The devotional narratives were inspired by the author's experiences as a court
    translator. But any similarity to actual persons, living or dead, or actual events,
    is purely coincidental. Information about names, ages, gender, and location
    have been modified to protect any and all individuals who inspired the
    narratives. Any similarity to a specific person or case is purely coincidental."

"No narrative is intended as legal advice and should not be taken as such.
    Neither are the specific references to the law to be considered as accurate
    representations of the law in any and all circumstances."

Printed in the United States of America.

Cover art by Zachariah James Stuef.

Dedication

To: Seb, Lola, Ethan, Leslie, Laura; Vince, Noah, Alan, Esther;
Jaylee Jill, Kristina, Tyler; Orlando Samuel, Mercedes Camacho;
Samuel Camacho, Bertilda Camacho; Alberto Samuel,
Elber Samuel, Betty Luz, all my nearest DNA family,
and my family of the heart; and to my extended family
in the gospel, whom I will only meet in the Kingdom
of the Son of God, Son of man, and through his grace alone.

Contents

Foreword

The apostle Paul's central thesis is that we cannot persist in relying on our own powers. Our condition, into which we are born, can never be anything but one of helplessness and conflict. As a consequence, there is only one way this can be halted. Jesus Christ must come to us.

This was Paul's experience, as we learn from his epistles. So long as Paul remained a Pharisee, even being the "Pharisee of Pharisees" as he claimed, he was trapped in a hopeless struggle. He knew as well as anyone God's commands and that he must live as a good and righteous man. But, despite his earnest desire to accomplish this, his efforts came to nothing.

Then Jesus Christ came to him. The God he prosecuted and persecuted revealed the truth to Paul, translating Paul into the kingdom of Christ and transforming and renewing the thoughts of his mind. Christ now ruled over Paul's life and the result was his old self was annihilated. Paul now differed in every way from the zealous Pharisee who clung to the law as a guide and goad for living a righteous life before God.

Paul underwent what so many, including the author of this book, have experienced: even when we live according to the tenets of God's commands and man's laws we are not strong enough to conquer our sinful hearts. As a consequence, we are reduced to pitiful creatures. Namely, that we recognize what we should do, and we genuinely want to do it, but we are incapable of sublimating our self-centeredness. In theological terms, that's what's meant by the Church's doctrine of original sin. We are sinners, which means we are inherently selfish and there's nothing we can do to reverse direction and become wholly selfless, as God demands of us. The tragedy of human existence then is that in our pursuit of a good and righteous life we become more and more selfish.

This book then, like St. Paul's epistles, has much to say about the old and new life; specifically how life and righteousness may be attained.

The only means for the attainment of life and righteousness is given by God as a free gift. Jesus Christ, not the law, accomplishes the impossible for us. Jesus' death and resurrection relieve us of the burden, the intolerable constraints of daily trying to live in such a way that we can prove ourselves worthy to stand before the living God and hear him say: Well done, good and faithful servant!

It is this radical proclamation that changes everything for us. Now there is no longer any talk of what we should do and leave undone. There is no longer any debate about obeying God's commands by exercising our willpower. Now that Christ is risen from the dead it is evident from the preaching of the Gospel and the administration of his gifts of salvation that only one principle is operative in the lives of Christians: the unforced, spontaneous love of God poured out upon us in abundance in and through Jesus Christ.

In this book then, the reader will discover evidence for Christ that demands no verdict. The author understands well that, despite the goodness of the law, it lays a terrible burden upon us. The law's demands that we live a good and righteous life drives us into troubles and perplexities, not because the law is pulling a bait and switch on us but because we are helpless to do what it commands. So, in a remarkably Pauline way, the author tells us this himself through a series of meditations taken from his own life, to relieve us of the terrible burden of the law, and comfort us with the Gospel of Jesus Christ. A Gospel that declares:

. . . at the right time, while we were still powerless, Christ died for the ungodly. Very rarely will anyone die for a righteous man, though for a good man someone might possibly dare to die. But God proves His love for us in this: While we were still sinners, Christ died for us (Romans 5:6-8).

In the Name + of Jesus,
Rev. Donavon L. Riley
July 18, 2022

Preface

For over twenty years I heard countless guilty verdicts, heightened by the blow of the judge's gavel. Every working day I served as a Certified Court Interpreter for the judicial system in the California courts. Sometimes we would hear over 100 criminal and civil matters in a single day! Some were minor traffic infractions, others misdemeanors, others were serious felonies. There were also countless divorce petitions, Stay-away orders, allegations of child abuse, and Juvenile Court matters. At the center of each allegation, there was a human being who at one time had been a newborn child, representing the innocence, curiosity, joy, and promise of human existence. Yet, years later here was that same person, accused of any one of many crimes: armed robbery, assault, murder, rape, and all types of sexual assault, physical and sexual abuse of minors, drug trafficking, breaking and entering, drunk driving, drug abuse of all kinds, white collar crime, the list was endless. The humanity of most defendants appeared to turn against others as helpless and hapless as themselves.

Courtroom appearances, from arraignments through pretrials, trials, and sentencing were all a grand display of humanity at its worst, and rarely, at its best. I also witnessed the judicial system at its best and worst. Justice after all is in the hands of imperfect people: judges, attorneys, clerks, and yes, even interpreters. Sometimes one was left to wonder if some judicial officers and other court officers were misguided by their own prejudices against the different, the stranger, the immigrant, and the helpless. But mostly, the law reigned. The law covers every minutia of criminal conduct and applies a corresponding punishment. But the written law is blind to tears of remorse, pleas for leniency, repentance, and promises of changed behavior. It seemed as if the unyielding nature of the law produced, at least in some, greater evil instead of repentance. I saw hearts grow colder and harder, in judges as well as in delinquents, under the suffocating demands of civil and criminal law.

In this little book you will find many of those narratives. However, there is but only one abiding story, the story of the Gospel. The short stories told here serve only as a megaphone to tell the greatest story arising from God's own courtroom, dictating its own verdict of grace over humanity. It is the Good News of God's astonishing initiative in Jesus Christ handing down verdicts of absolution to guilty sinners, but at a great cost—the voluntary incarnation of God's only Son, Jesus Christ. He became our substitute in his life, death, and resurrection. Through Christ's completed work, God was able to dictate grace instead of condemnation, forgiveness instead of sentencing to guilty sinners, entirely through God's grace in Christ alone, and by faith alone. Each narrative moves from the unyielding dictates of human law to the courtroom before the presence of God, where the law is even more unbending. That is why Jesus Christ voluntarily became flesh so that the full weight of God's law would fall upon him. That way sinners receive grace and mercy through the life and sacrifice of Christ.

Some may see too much grace in the gospel story as told here, and I sincerely hope that is the case. Paraphrasing Luther's Preface to his Commentary on Galatians, "I formulated these narratives only for the perturbed, the afflicted, the tempted (the only ones who can understand such grace), those who are despondent in their faith. Those who need more instruction on how to live a pious life, might as well go to other books, with better narratives of self-improvement, and proven steps for defeating evil in all aspects of life, for they are legion."[1]

My gratitude to Mercedes, my wife, the prime motivator encouraging me to put these stories in writing, Thanks also to my eleven-year-old son, Orlando, who daily teaches me what it means to issue and receive our own daily verdicts of forgiveness. But this little book is for you, the reader. Make it yours. Draw on it, highlight it, read it

---

[1] Martin Luther's Commentary on Saint Paul's Epistle to the Galatians (1535), xix. Translated by Haroldo Camacho, 1517 Publishing, 2018.

alone or with loved ones every day, memorize Bible texts that jump out at you, copy them by hand, put them on your digital screens, tweet them, make them your own comfort. For God's verdict over you, the guilty one, has pounded a booming "Not Guilty" decree! All charges have been dropped. Your record is clean. Christ has taken your place in life and death, and so, "You are *eternally* forgiven."

January 22, 2022
Davie, Florida

1
The Judge Who Didn't Play Fair

> "This righteousness of God comes through faith in Jesus Christ for all . . . *It was* to demonstrate His righteousness at the present time, so that He would be just and the One who justifies those who have faith in Jesus" (Romans 3:22,26 AMP).

Sooner or later most drivers will receive an RSVP invitation to Traffic Court. They must answer guilty or not guilty to an infraction of one or more traffic laws. But it is the judge who sets the fine. Depending on the presiding judge on any particular day, the fine may vary, even if it's for the same infraction. Running a light could be as much as $425.00 USD, whereas another judge may impose a fine as low as $125.00. Rolling through a stop sign could be as high as $280.00, or as low as $100.00. Speeding: one judge imposes up to $450.00, another $225.00. Repeat offenders don't know what to expect. One day, it seems the judge overcharges. Another judge will cut it down in half. If there is no permanent judge sitting on the bench, it's what you'd call "the luck of the draw." Working as an interpreter at the courts, I've heard more than one defendant respond, "But Your Honor, the judges here don't play fair! One charges one thing, the other charges more for the same."

You can imagine this does not go well with the judge, who usually responds with, "And who said we're playing games here! It's you who's playing with people's lives and your own by driving forty miles over the speed limit!" What seems to be an injustice is all within the playing field. The legislature mandates the fines, but the judge is free to exercise his or her own judicial discretion within certain limits. There is nothing unfair about it. What seems unfair is after all a fair and level playing field. The appeal to unfairness falls on the deaf ears of the law. The written law does not have the discretion to lower or increase fines. The law does not have the power to forgive or absolve. Only the judge is able to exonerate a fine, decrease it, or increase it! Only the judge is able to reduce infractions or throw them out altogether.

But before the judgment seat of God, matters are entirely predictable. Only the supreme Judge of the universe is able to forgive, wipe records clean, or declare the wicked righteous. No similarities here to earthly tribunals. The fine, the punishment, is always the same, and for everyone. In that, the Judge has no discretion. "For the wages of sin is death" (Romans 6:23 ESV). Everyone must pay the maximum penalty: eternal death. There's no arguing, no pleading, no appealing to non-existing exculpatory footnotes in God's Law. But there is a Substitute. In divine justice, the sentence is handed to another. God's own Son, Jesus Christ, declares before the Judge: "I already paid that fine on the cross, for all the infractions, misdemeanors, felonies, and high crimes. Completely. I paid the last cent over 2,000 years ago. I took the place of every sinner, and all who believe me have their penalty paid in full." Scripture calls this marvelous exchange "the righteousness of God." On the cross God took off your load of every single sin and placed it on Christ. Then, He heaped on you the fullness of His holiness and perfection. "For in Him dwells all the fullness of the Godhead bodily; and you are complete in Him" (Colossians 2:9,10 NKJV). "This righteousness is given through faith in Jesus Christ to all who believe . . . to demonstrate his righteousness at the present time, so as to be just and the one who justifies those who have faith in Jesus" (Romans 3:22,26 NIV). But this does indeed seem like the Judge is not playing fair.

Why? Because you are entirely forgiven, freely, without paying even a microscopic amount of a red or white blood cell! It is totally just and fair because that punishment was paid on your behalf, on someone else's body. It was paid on a body who loves you, someone who cannot live without you. He did the unthinkable; He took your nasty stuff on his spotless soul. We merited nothing but punishment, abandonment, and death. But the eternal Judge used His judicial discretion, and in Christ removed your guilt and sentence of death. It always drops my jaw, that due to God's sheer pure and unmerited grace, we were loved and declared righteous, holy, and perfect in His sight. We can only trust in His completed work on our behalf. If we trust our feelings to provide the evidence that it's true, we will be disappointed. At times we will feel like we are still covered with a lot of muck, and with more than one sin hanging around. Yet when God looks at our computer file and searches for "sin," the search comes back: "None seen." The only thing that shows up in our file is the perfect life of His Son Jesus Christ.

Do you believe this? Confess it with your mouth and believe it in your heart. You have been embraced in God's arms, cleansed by His grace. You are loved and cared for in His embrace forever.

2

The Divorce Never Decreed

"I will never leave you nor forsake you . . ." "Fear not, for
I am with you. Do not be dismayed. I am your God. I will
strengthen you; I will help you; I will uphold you with my
victorious right hand" (Hebrews 13:5; NKJV Isaiah 41:10 ESV).

When the Family Court judge called the next name on the calendar,
an elderly couple slowly made their way to the table. Each one sat on
either end. I took my place in the middle as their interpreter before
the judge in the proceedings. Both had basically the same appearance. The skin on their arms, hands, and face was toasted and wrinkled, most certainly the marks of years of working under the hot
California sun, in the agricultural fields. Their faces looked like they
had not broken a smile for a long time, probably due to hardships
beyond our comprehension. Their faces yielded no emotional clues,
as they looked expressionless toward the judge. It was he who broke
the silence. "Mr. Francisco, this is your plea to terminate your marriage of thirty-nine years. Have you already come to an agreement
with Ms. Matilde as to the details of the settlement, or do you wish
for me to hear the matter and pronounce on the issues?" I translated
faithfully and precisely but somewhat fearful that the couple might
not understand his legalese.

But he answered clearly and deliberately, "Yes, Your Honor,
we've already come to an agreement."

The judge followed with, "What then is the agreement? Do you
have something in writing?"

A profound silence ensued as the old gentleman searched his wrinkled hands for an answer. Then he spoke up, again clearly and methodically. "Your Honor, it's that we no longer want a divorce."

I immediately translated into English. The judge was taken aback and responded in honest amazement but directing his question toward the woman. "Is that true, madam? You no longer want a divorce?"

"Yes, Your Honor," she replied without hesitation. We talked about it. We're going to keep on living together." The judge quickly withdrew the man's plea for divorce. The couple rose as old folk do: carefully pushed back and stood leaning their weight on the table. Their thick and wrinkled hands found each other. Walking hands together, and moving with the ungainliness of their years, they slowly walked away and past the double doors of the courtroom.

Ever since our first parents implied that somehow God was to blame for what "the serpent" did to them, humanity has constantly pressed for a divorce from God. It has come up with heady, yet seemingly persuasive arguments. "God does not really exist, God is dead, if God does exist, God is cruel and unjust, God allows way too much suffering, poverty, and death. The Bible contains nothing but myths. I believe in evolution, not in the creation story. It's up to humankind to save itself. Should God exist, God cannot forgive my sins, they are too many, too persistent, and way too offensive." But on the cross, Christ took our place on that cross, and with His own plea, He cried out, "I will not divorce you; I will not let you divorce me; I love you; I love you way too much, I love you forever. I love you so much I have died for you." Our senseless divorce plea is drowned out by the voice of our Groom Jesus Christ who cries out, "I will never forsake you or abandon you . . . Do not fear: I am with you; do not be anxious: I am your God, I will strengthen you, I will help you, I will uphold you with my victorious right hand" (Hebrews 13:5 CSB; Isaiah 41:10 ESV). For God, neither our unbelief nor our unfaithfulness, nor perversity nor indifference is a cause for divorce. On the cross, Christ paid the price for all our sins and gave us the most precious pearl as a wedding present: His own righteousness! This perfect righteousness is our wedding garment. "I will greatly rejoice in the Lord, my whole being shall exult in my God; for he has clothed me with the garments of salvation, he has covered me with the robe of righteousness" (Isaiah 61:10 NRSV).

Ultimately, we will all find ourselves at God's judgment seat (2 Corinthians 5:10). However, there will be no divorce decree. The Judge will say: "It's unwarranted, no judicial cause on account of Christ's plea." Then, Jesus our Groom, with His nail-scarred hands takes our hands and walks out with us from that ultimate courtroom, and into eternity – His eternity – and a never-ending wedding feast. It's celebrated with bread and wine in infinite supply. There is no hushed courtroom here. The great multitude exclaims, "To the one seated on the throne and to the Lamb be blessing and honor and glory and might forever and ever!" (Revelation 5:13 NRSV).

3

Seeing Stars

> And he brought him outside and said, "Look toward heaven, and number the stars, if you are able to number them." Then he said to him, "So shall your offspring be." And he believed the Lord, and he counted it to him as righteousness (Genesis 15:5,6 ESV).

For many years, I also worked as a certified court interpreter at the Mental Health Court in Los Angeles, California. One of the most frequent hearings was to determine mental competency in detained individuals. A judge may determine that a person may be held under the supervision of the mental health court. The loss of one's liberty may be temporary or indefinite. If it is deemed indefinite, the person is placed in what is called a Conservatorship. Once a year, there's a review of that person's condition and the case is brought before the judge for a ruling. The judge may rule that the person has recovered sufficiently to return to society. But first, an attorney interviews the client/patient and follows up with a recommendation to the judge. The clients also make every effort to be well prepared for these hearings. It's a once-a-year opportunity to recover their rights and freedom.

I remember a particular interview. A man had been admitted through a 5150 (emergency mental health detention) to a mental health institution. He showed symptoms of a psychotic breakdown, diagnosed as schizophrenia. The man alleged to see stars, galaxies, entire constellations of galaxies projected on walls, ceilings, plain daylight, people's foreheads, or practically any place. He would relate to these objects as if they were his only reality and ignore his own. He would walk out into the street without care for traffic, talking to the stars. He would ignore care for his own body because he lived in another dimension. Before his illness, astronomy had been his hobby. He could name many stars, galaxies, and give their precise location as well as other characteristics. But now it was a psychotic obsession, and he could no longer concentrate on anything else.

However, during the interview with the attorney, the patient denied having had any of these experiences during the past months. He claimed to have taken his medications regularly. He seemed well oriented as to time and space, and his responses to the attorney corresponded to the questions. There was not a hint of galactic troubles. The recommendation from the psychiatrist was also positive. The attorney congratulated him, adding that he was recommending immediate release. The man was ecstatic. The attorney was the first to exit the interview room. As I prepared to leave, the man touched my elbow and called out softly to me. "Sir!" He said with a look and tone of wonderment. "How do you get Orion to jump from one of your legs to the other?"

The attorney heard the murmur, turned around, and inquired, "What did the guy just say?"

Obviously, he was seeing stars. But on a certain occasion many years ago, Abraham, the father of faith, was also seeing stars. He was even counting them! Wasn't that even crazier? And besides, he was also hearing God talking to him. Call the 5150 team, please. He even heard that his One Seed would be more numerous than all those stars put together. But, "Abraham believed God, and it was counted to him as righteousness" (Genesis 15:6 Brenton).

Now, that's having lost it altogether! If Abraham had been a man of science today, perhaps the Biblical story would read differently. He might have asked certain pertinent questions that would have made more sense than just "believing"! He might have asked, "Well, that's all the stars I can see, but perhaps there are some more stars forming within those galactic clouds? Then I can be sure I've counted them all. And what about the microwave background radiation? Are there any stars hiding there? And doesn't that prove the Big Bang theory rather than the outdated mythological creation story? And then another question: Those stars are the ones I can count now, but they only represent stars from thousands of light years ago. How many have been born since then? I want to know the how, when, and how many . . . exactly. And please don't forget to explain the expansion of the universe. Is it eventually going to go dark? Certainly, a modern Abraham would want all those scientific questions answered correctly before believing that an "outside, foreign righteousness" would be counted as his. To do otherwise would be reason for a 5150.

But the way God declares sinners righteous on the basis of grace through faith goes beyond mathematical calculations and astronomical observations. "For the foolishness of God is wiser than human wisdom, and the weakness of God is stronger than human strength" (1 Corinthians 1:25 NIV). In other words, there's more sanity in God's 5150 than in all human mental competency. And what is God's 5150? The foolishness of the Gospel! To believe – against all evidence to the contrary within us – that sinners are declared righteous by God's word alone. To a believing sinner that's nothing more than seeing stars, galaxies, and galaxy clusters jumping all over the place! And through that insanity is how God restores humanity to full sanity, forever, without a shadow of a doubt. The only evidence? The blood of Christ shed on Calvary's cross, not for Himself but for insane sinners who live between mud puddles and the clouds. This is the sanest insanity we may hope for. And although according to human wisdom it may be deemed 5150 worthy, "in accordance with his promise, we wait for new heavens and a new earth, where righteousness is at home" (2 Peter 3:13 NRSV). From what galaxy to what galaxy are you now jumping for joy?

4

When The "Cold Ones" Burn You

> "For there is one God, and there is one mediator between God and men, the man Christ Jesus, who gave himself as a ransom for all" (1 Timothy 2:5,6 ESV).

All too frequently, I've had to translate for the sentencing of drunk drivers. I remember the words of a defendant after the judge's ruling: "Those cold ones burned me." Regularly, a "six" costs some six dollars, a "12 pack" some nine bucks. But when the defendant is sentenced for drunk driving, those "cold ones" really burn you. In this instance, he got burned with a $3,654.00 dollar fine. The district attorney was explaining the sentence. "The fine for driving under the influence the first time is $1,660.00. But there are other fees and surcharges. $434.08 for booking, $150.00 for damages, $500.00 for an ankle bracelet for thirty days of house arrest, $540 for a nine-month drunk drivers prevention program, $300.00 for high blood alcohol level. A total of $3,654.08!" When this regular guy savored those "cold ones," he never thought he'd get burned with $3,654.08 for the pleasure of having "a few" with his friends on that Friday night. But that wasn't all the bad news for this defendant.

No sooner had the judge sentenced him than the district attorney went on. "Your Honor, this defendant has a second DUI. He was also arrested on the following Sunday coming back from a birthday party. By the time the district attorney added up all fines and fees for both DUIs, he'd gotten burned with a grand total of $7,308.16 US." There was no defense. In the first, his blood alcohol had been .19 percent, in the second, .26 percent, over three times the legal limit! He would have to pay both fines in three years at $203.00 a month. He earned only $800.00 a month working in the agricultural fields. However, he had to provide for his wife, himself, and three children under six.

But the "cold ones" were not done burning. As soon as the judge handed down the ruling for the second DUI, the district attorney spoke up again. "Your Honor, this man is a menace to himself and to others. His second DUI proves he has no respect for the law. I request he be denied home detention and comply with his sixty-day jail sentence locked up in the county jail."

"Granted," was the judge's only response. The deputies quickly cuffed him. Just then, an attractive young woman got up and headed for the courtroom exit. A strapping young man about her age followed her out the door. I wasn't the only to notice. The defendant whispered to me, "Would you find out for me who that dude is with my wife?" What he saw was the last burn.

As the "cold ones" burned him one after another, none of his drinking buddies were in court to comfort him, much less offer to pay his fine or to find out "who that dude was with his wife." As his public defender told him, "Where are your drinking buddies to put their hands in the fire for you right now?"

But in God's judgment hall, He does not see anyone as hopeless, pointless, impenitent, or irredeemable. "For there is one God, and one mediator between God and men, the man Christ Jesus, who gave himself as a ransom for all . . . God was in Christ reconciling the world unto Himself, not taking into account our sins . . . Him who knew no sin was made sin for us, so that we might be made the righteousness of God in Him" (1 Timothy 2:5,6 ESV; 2 Corinthians 5:19-21 ERV). It's easy to feel that "righteous indignation" at the drunk driver before the judge, and say within ourselves that "he had it coming to him," or "lucky thing he didn't get killed"; but in the end and before God's judgment seat, we're all the same. God does indeed look upon the heart, and what's there is not pretty. What he wants to find is missing. We lack mercy, grace, kindness, even toward our loved ones and dearest friends. We get upset over the slightest frustrations, berating others under our breath. We always want to come out on top, and when we embarrass ourselves, we blame others. We are drunk on our own egos and selfishness. But God offers His abundant and overflowing grace to the drunk driver as well as to us. This gift is given to us in the perfect love, purity, and holiness of His Son Jesus Christ. It is yours and mine entirely by faith alone. It's a matter of letting go of what we want to give Him (even our hearts), and having bare and empty hands (and heart) to receive His great gift of forgiveness and righteousness. He is the one that came at the moment when the sentence was handed down and put His hands in the fire for us, there at the judgment seat of the cross, where we were all declared guilty. But on the cross, He also took our place as the righteous one, and instead of condemnation we were handed down forgiveness, instead of punishment, we were set free. Even though we may deem ourselves the worst of sinners, by faith alone He declares us righteous forever without stain or wrinkle before God. Why? Because He loves us passionately, and His will for us is eternal life with Him. Confess your faith in His perfect love for you, no matter how many DUIs of sin you may have in your record. His Holy Spirit will grant you repentance, and all of Christ's life will be counted as yours, forever!

5

My Mom's Never Gonna Forgive Me!

> "He was crushed for the guilt our sins deserved. The punishment that brought us peace was upon him, and by his wounds we are healed. We all have gone astray like sheep. Each of us has turned to his own way, but the Lord has charged all our guilt to him" (Isaiah 53:4-6 NIV).

She was right. Her mom never forgave her. I was translating to the minor the words of the public defender. He wanted to convince her that if she behaved in the foster home, she could return home sooner rather than later under the supervision of her own mother. The girl was only fifteen, but she was already deep into drugs. Her mother caught her rummaging through her purse. When mom scolded her, the girl picked up a large frying skillet and brought it down on her mother's head with all her might. The woman instantly fell unconscious to the floor. The girl ran to the next-door neighbor screaming that her mother had a heart attack. But the evidence pointed in another direction. The girl had lard in her hands, the same kind that was still stuck to the frying pan. And the horrible bump on her mother's head? The charges leveled against the minor were serious felonies. Attempted murder, grave bodily injuries. But since she was a minor and this was her first case, the charges were reduced to a misdemeanor, simple battery. She would be released after six months on probation, and sooner if she were willing to return to her home, and her mother would agree to supervise her.

"But my mom's never gonna forgive me," she protested.

"Don't think that way," countered her attorney. "She has a mother's heart."

"But you don't know my mother; she's not gonna forgive me. And after all, what happened is her fault 'cause she didn't want to give me the money."

When the attorney and I spoke to the mother, she told us, "It's that I can no longer control her; there's nothing else I can do for her. She's completely out of control." Then, without shedding a tear, she signed the document waving her parental rights over her daughter, effective immediately and forever.

The attorney sat there looking at the document as if searching for words that would make it disappear. "It's that I've never seen a case quite like this, madam."

The mother retorted, "It's that you've never seen someone quite like my daughter."

It was a long, slow walk back to the courtroom where the judge was waiting to hear the mother's petition to perpetually waive her parental rights. The judge's words were not welcoming. "So, what kind of mother would waive her parental rights forever?"

The mother didn't hesitate. "The kind of mother who wants to save my daughter's life, as well as my own. If she comes back to me, she'll kill me. Then you'd have a dead body to bury, and a minor to put away for life. I did all I could. Lock her up for a long time, Your Honor. She'd even kill you for drugs if she had a chance."

The minor was present at the hearing. I was translating for both mother and daughter, mother behind, daughter in front. The girl stood before the judge guarded by two bailiffs, one on either side. Her hands were cuffed behind her back. However, both middle fingers on each hand were raised in a defiant obscenity. The judge couldn't see the obscene gesture obviously directed at the mother, but it fully confirmed her mother's words. The district attorney, who had been observing the entire proceeding a few steps back, immediately requested a private conference with the judge at the bar. It was brief. Without further delay, the judge granted the mother's request.

We must not dare think we're any better than this girl. In our immaturity, we are addicted to our own selfishness, greed, lust, and anger, to name a few of our addictions. We then let go of all that fury against Him who loved us, and loved us to the end. We put Him on a cross, and just like the girl, we blamed Him for our sin: "You made us this way. After all, we're your children. You didn't create us quite right."

But He won't tire of us. His heart is a father and mother's heart toward us, and He will never waive His parental right to love us, care for us, and see us safe to eternity. He has seen the worst of all, and most painfully, He saw it in His very own Son, for He made Him to be made sin for us. And because of that great sacrifice, He has already welcomed us home in Christ's resurrection and ascension. He has seen all our obscene gestures, but His response was the gesture of His nail-pierced hands and feet. In Christ, we're already being loved at His side. "Surely he has borne our grief and carried our sorrows; yet we esteemed him stricken, smitten by God, and afflicted. But he was wounded for our transgressions, he was bruised for our iniquities; upon him was the chastisement that made us whole, and with his stripes we are healed. All we like sheep have gone astray; we have turned everyone to his own way; and the Lord has laid on him the iniquity of us all (Isaiah 53:4-6 NKJV). We can vent all our fury on Him, blaspheme Him, deny His existence, make light of "the whole crucifixion thing," consider the Biblical story as just another ancient myth. But what God has done in Christ, is a *fait accompli;* it has been done, and cannot be undone by you, me, or anyone else, including God Himself. Christ has already answered on our behalf, and today He loves us forever! If you think God "is never gonna forgive me," then you don't know Christ. If we think "Christ's death did nothing for me," then we don't know the Father. If we come up to God's judgment seat with a petition for Him to waive His Creator and paternal rights over us, He'll only pull us to Him and hold us in His eternal embrace.

6

Unexpected Grace

> "The Spirit of the Lord is on me, because he anointed me to preach good news to the poor. He has sent me to proclaim freedom to the captives and recovery of sight to the blind, to set free those who are oppressed, and to proclaim the year of the Lord's favor!" (Luke 4:18,19 HCSB).

I lived through many moments of great suspense when I worked as a translator in the courtrooms. But the most dramatic, suspense filled moments are when a jury enters the courtroom after concluding its deliberations. A group of twelve people have been huddled together for hours, sometimes many days, carefully studying every shred of evidence presented against the defendant. Only those who have lived those moments know first-hand the agony of awaiting the verdict. Even if you are not the defendant, you feel the tension in the air. In a few seconds, the defendant will know what the future will hold. Whether it will be spending years in jail, or whether he will be released to glorious freedom. If we can enter that defendant's head, this is probably what he's thinking: "If the jury's verdict is 'Not Guilty,' what awaits me is the warmth of my home, the tight embrace of my wife and children, and the raucous welcome of my friends and family. But if the jury's verdict is 'Guilty,' I'll be sent off to the loneliness of prison far from my family, surrounded by dangerous criminals who will most likely welcome me with the worst beating of my life!"

On a particular day, the defendant was a young man, about twenty-five years old. He had been accused of voluntary manslaughter.

The district attorney's evidence and her arguments did not appear overwhelmingly convincing, or in legalese, "beyond a reasonable doubt." There had been several gang members involved in the shooting. The defendant claimed he was just an innocent passer-by during the incident. Further, that the police indiscriminately stopped him. He didn't have the telltale signs of gunpowder in his hands. Yet, an empty 9-millimeter handgun had been found in his car. The young man did not have the funds to hire a private attorney and investigators, but he had always held out hope for a "Not Guilty" verdict. His attorney had presented a strong defense, which he hoped had created reasonable doubt in the majority of the jury. But when the ruling came down, it hit him with tsunami force: "Guilty."

As I translated the verdict, he sat with his hands in his face, trying to hold back the tears. He was later sentenced to eight years in the state penitentiary, with a chance for parole in six. An older woman from the community who had been following the case surprisingly showed up in prison a few days later to visit him. "I brought your wife and children to visit you. You have permission to visit with them for a few hours."

"But who are you, and why are you doing this?" asked the surprised young man.

"That doesn't matter; don't waste your time thinking about that. Your family is waiting for your visit." The unexpected benefactor was always faithful and throughout the ensuing months and years, always went to visit him, bringing along his wife and children. He was able to see his children grow, sustain his relationship with his wife, and keep up with news from his extended family and friends. After six years, he was granted parole and returned back home to the joyous welcome he had always imagined. The benefactor had a job waiting for him, and today he is a useful member of society and his community. The benefactor has made him and his family part of her extended family, and the young man and his family consider her as their "other mom."

A little over two thousand years ago, an unexpected young man presented Himself to the human family and proclaimed, "The Spirit of the Lord is upon me, because he has anointed me to proclaim good news to the poor. He has sent me to proclaim freedom for the prisoners and recovery of sight for the blind, to set the oppressed free, to proclaim the year of the Lord's favor" (Luke 4:18,19 HCSB). This unknown, unexpected young man not only came to visit and comfort the human family with his compassion for the poor, the abandoned, the sick. He came to take our place as the death sentence came down upon us in the jailhouse of death. Yes, the death sentence had already been handed down to us, in fact to every single person who has ever breathed and will breathe upon the planet. There had been no jury deliberations. It was the sentence of the Judge of the Universe, according to the power of the Law to condemn for all transgressions, even those that we may think occur only in the imagination. But with the power of His "not-guiltiness," He busted wide open the iron doors of death's prison, tore up the writ of our condemnation. Then, He did the unthinkable. He replaced it with the record of His own pure, perfectly obedient, loving life! But that's not all. With the power of His resurrection, He opened infinitely wide the gates of heaven, never again to be closed shut to any believing human being, regardless of social class, race, gender, or place of origin.

Today by faith, we can live free from guilt, free from the fear of death, free from all slander the devil could whisper and scatter about us. In Him, we have a new family, the family of the forgiven. His visit two thousand years ago took us by surprise with this Good News: "I'm here to be with you. I'm here to bring you to your new family. I bring to you fresh bread for your spirit, pure and eternal water to quench your spiritual thirst. Look, I'm opening the jail doors, come out, come with me. Come; follow me. And oh yes, I've also got a great job for you. Not to pay me back for what I've done. You could never do that. Just for your delight and satisfaction: Tell others what great things God has done for you."

7

The [almost] Forgiven Crime

"I, yes I, am he. I blot out your rebellious deeds for my own sake, and I will not remember your sins . . . Who is a God like you, who pardons sin and forgives the transgression . . . You do not stay angry forever but delight to show mercy. You will again have compassion on us; you will tread our sins underfoot and hurl all our iniquities into the depths of the sea" (Isaiah 43:25 NET; Micah 7:18-19 NIV).

The courtroom was full. Visitors were ushered out. There was room only for defendants. The public defender took her place to instruct the accused. I stood by her side and translated simultaneously. At the end, she added: "There's a program offered by the District Attorney for those who wish to take advantage of it. It's a way of getting this offense off your record. It's called Delayed Sentencing Program. If you plead guilty today to the charges, go to a class for six hours, pay a fine, and avoid any run ins with the law for the next three months, this charge is taken off your record for good. Puff! Gone! Except, listen now." (I knew what was coming so I was prepared to follow her.) "If you are an undocumented alien, you don't have any papers to prove your residency in this country, or if you are not a citizen, it doesn't matter if you go to the program. The charges are dismissed as far as the state, but not for the federal government. Since you have pleaded guilty to a misdemeanor, you will still have problems with immigration. The charges will still appear in your record. If you fall in that category, it's better NOT to go to the program. Instead, tell the judge you want to speak to a public defender before pleading guilty to the charges." In other words, the record would *almost* be wiped clean.

During the course of the morning, a certain young man was called to answer for the charge of driving without a license. The district attorney had already offered him the Delayed Sentencing Program. But the defendant had been paying attention to the translated instructions. When the judge asked him how he pled to the charge, he answered, "I want to talk to a public defender."

She took the file, briefly looked over it, and then answered, "Your Honor, I request this charge be dismissed because it was filed beyond the statute of limitations." What she meant is that the district attorney had delayed for more than a year before filing the charge. Therefore, according to the law, the charge must be dismissed. Puff! Gone! The judge confirmed the date, and threw out the charges.

The defendant just stood there not quite sure of what had just happened. The public defender just looked at him and said, "Hurry up and leave the courtroom, now!" I translated as quickly as I could. The astonished man slowly realized the fortunate turn of events. He thanked me, told me to thank the attorney, the judge; he thanked God, wished everyone along the hallway a great day, and left with a spring in his step. He had been defended by the attorney. Protected by the law. Forgiven by the judge. There were no state or federal charges. He walked out of the courtroom a forgiven man.

When we appear before the judgment seat of God, the law accuses us, not just of committing one or two sins. Instead, its records show that all of our life has been one of "trespasses and sins." In fact, that our very nature loves nothing but sin, and hates the law and God Himself. All of these are punishable by the death sentence. But the eternal Judge took all our sins and condemned them not in our body, but in the body of Christ. He was condemned, sentenced, and punished so that our record would be wiped entirely clean. Thus, because of Christ and His sacrifice, there is no more record of our sins, neither of those we think are insignificant or the most perverse. Scripture says, "He destroyed the record of the debt we owed, with its requirements that worked against us. He canceled it by nailing it to the cross" (Colossians 2:14 CEB). Further, "I, even I, am He who blots out your transgressions for My own sake; And I will not remember your sins" (Isaiah 43:25 ESV). That's not all: "He will again have compassion on us; he will trample our iniquities. And you will hurl all their sins in the depths of the sea" (Micah 7:19 NLT).

On the cross, and from within Christ's innocent being, God heard our prayer. Given so much grace, do we want to grasp this pardon, or would we rather work the delayed sentencing program and have our sins *almost* forgiven? We will have to pay every last cent, work the program perfectly, and then live with the assurance that we have *not* been totally forgiven. But if we grasp by faith that blessed pardon, we will live an eternal life of gratefulness. Further, right now we will finally be able to hurl other's offenses also into the depths of the sea (where God has already thrown our own). There is no greater freedom than to forgive and forget. And God lives in that freedom through the finished work of Christ. With God there is no *almost forgiven*, because at the cross, all our sins and trespasses, and all that arises from our sinful nature was blotted out once and for all. We now live in the blessed paradise of the forgiven.

8

It Wasn't Me, It Was Somebody Else

> "He does not treat us as our sins deserve or repay us according to our iniquities. For as high as the heavens are above the earth, so great is his love for those who fear him; as far as the east is from the west, so far has he removed our transgressions from us" (Psalm 103:10-12 NIV).

He was only nineteen years old. He'd come to the United States full of hopes and ambitions. After just a few weeks, he already had a part time job. But now he was detained, dressed in the jail issued orange jump suit. He'd been brought up to the courtroom, cuffed and shackled. Today was his preliminary hearing, and it was his opportunity to tell his story to his attorney (as I translated). On the night of the incident, he could not fall asleep. He heard rustling noises outside his window. He remembered it was a full moon, and the night was clear. As he looked outside, he saw that someone was breaking into the neighbor's house through an open window. Alarmed, he climbed out of his own window and climbed up and over the window left open by the thief in the house next door. He wanted to catch him in the act. Meanwhile, the man of the house woke up. He'd heard noises downstairs and immediately called 911. The thief panicked and fled through the back door. The young man chased after him but stumbled on a chair and fell. He broke a couple of toes and twisted his ankle. That quickly halted his chase. Just then the police arrived and caught him in the neighbor's house, *infraganti* (red-handed), with an open window nearby and his soiled footprints on the floor. Damning evidence.

Regardless of his persistent protests to the contrary and his story that he'd just been chasing the real thief, he was arrested in his boxer shorts for trespassing, breaking and entering an inhabited dwelling. The charge amounted to a serious felony, punishable by up to twelve years in prison. The police had been so confident they had their man that they had not even bothered to look for other fingerprints in the window. "But it wasn't me; it was somebody else. I just wanted to catch him. I was just chasing him, almost had him, and now the real thief is laughing at me and the police 'cause he got away. Believe me," he insisted to the attorney, "it wasn't me; it was somebody else. I just wanted to catch him. Believe me, believe, don't doubt it. I just wanted to do something good and catch the guy. Look, I was arrested in my boxer shorts."

His defense attorney, of course, assured him that, indeed, he believed him. "However," he added, "what's important is that the jury believes you when you tell them your story in trial."

But before the heavenly judgment seat, there is another who makes a totally different declaration. "It was I; it wasn't you!" The Son of God, Jesus the Christ takes the blame upon Himself so that you and I can be declared entirely "Not Guilty." "For Christ also suffered once for sins, the righteous for the unrighteous, to bring you to God. He was put to death in the body but made alive in the Spirit" (1 Peter 3:18 NIV). "The Lord is compassionate and gracious, slow to anger, abounding in love. He will not always accuse, nor will he harbor his anger forever; he does not treat us as our sins deserve or repay us according to our iniquities. For as high as the heavens are above the earth, so great is his love for those who fear him; as far as the east is from the west, so far has he removed our transgressions from us. As a father has compassion on his children, so the Lord has compassion on those who fear him; for he knows how we are formed, he remembers that we are dust" (Psalm 103:8-14 NIV).

It's somebody else who accuses us, the accuser of our brothers (Revelation 12:10). But when Jesus of Nazareth took our place on the cross, He took from our hands our guilty verdict, and placed it on Himself. That verdict, which for us was our shame, was His badge of honor. "But he was pierced for our transgressions, he was crushed for our iniquities, the punishment that brought us peace was on him, and by his wounds we are healed" (Isaiah 53:5 NIV). Thus, today God in

Christ says to you and me: "It was I; it wasn't you, believe me, believe me, don't ever doubt it. I have taken your place. The evidence is my cross, my shed blood. That cannot be undone. I did it for you, once and for all. The guilty verdict will never again be placed in your hands. It has been once and for all taken off your record. I declare you free, righteous, holy, and good. Forever." "If you, Lord, kept a record of sins, Lord, who could stand? But with you there is forgiveness, so that we can, with reverence, serve you" (Psalms 130:3-4 NIV).

9

Why Was The Judge So Angry?

> "For God did not send his Son into the world to condemn
> the world, but to save the world through him. Whoever
> believes in him is not condemned, but whoever does not
> believe stands condemned already because they have
> not believed in the name of God's one and only Son"
> (John 3:17-18 NIV).

It never ceases to amaze me. The good news is always harder to believe than the bad news. There are certain criminal charges that can be dismissed on the spot by the judge. Most of those are because the District Attorney failed to file charges in a timely manner. When these defendants come before the judge, there's one great piece of good news that awaits them. "On his own motion, the judge dismisses the matter due to expiration of the statute of limitations."

But the accused has his mind on his own guilt. On this particular day, the defendant whispered to me, "I knew what I did would catch up with me sooner or later. But tell the judge that I'm going to pay for everything now, with interest; maybe he'll let me go and won't lock me up." But the judge simply responds that he's using his own authority to dismiss the charges. He's free to go. However, the defendant is only paying attention to his own sense of guilt. He whispers to me again, "Tell the judge I'm gonna pay, to just give me another chance."

My obligation is to translate everything the defendant says. But when the judge hears me, he gets somewhat upset. "Tell the defendant that I already dismissed the charges. He's free to go now."

But the man does not budge. "Your Honor, what's the total then that I need to pay?"

That's when the judge lost it. "Look, mister. You have no charges against you! Leave the courtroom now; there's nothing pending against you!"

"But tell the judge I'm working now, and I can pay the whole thing."

"What?" (The judge is now visibly angry, and the tone of his voice is restrained anger.) "What didn't you understand about 'there are no charges against you'? What's wrong with you? Do you really want me to lock you up?"

"No, Your Honor. That's why I want to pay."

Finally, the judge can't take it anymore. "Bailiff! Get this guy out of the courtroom now before I lock him up for contempt of a court order. One more word from him, and I'm going to lock him up for disobeying a court order!"

God's word has a similar message but with eternal consequences for us. The judge of all says: "I, even I, am he who blots out your transgressions, for my own sake, and remembers your sins no more" (Isaiah 43:25 NIV). On the cross, in the body of Jesus, God kept His promise. In the broken body of the God-man Jesus, our sins were totally blotted out. He willingly took our sins on His body, suffered the sentence of eternal death on our behalf. Then, the Father on His own initiative issued His word of pardon over us. But, do we believe the Supreme Judge? Do we believe His word of forgiveness through the blood of His Son, or do we keep on asking how much we still owe Him? "For God did not send his Son into the world to condemn the world, but to save the world through him. Whoever believes in him is not condemned, but whoever does not believe stands condemned already because they have not believed in the name of God's one and only Son" (John 3:17-18 NIV).

The Judge's wrath is not because of what you did, but because when He tells you He's forgiven you, you don't believe Him. Not believing His word –"forgiven"– is our worst sin. He gave His Son, and the Son gave Himself for our forgiveness. God rejoices when we believe His word, "Forgiven," because then the sacrifice of the Son was not in vain for us. It was God's great gift to save us from our unbelief. Let us receive that word of freedom, unless we'd rather lock ourselves up forever!

10

The Happiest Day

> "Because you are his sons, God sent the Spirit of his Son into our hearts, the Spirit who calls out, "Abba, Father." So you are no longer a slave, but God's child; and since you are his child, God has made you also an heir" (Galatians 4:6-7 NIV).

Three children walked into the courtroom. Their innocent laughter transformed the somber mood of the hall. Their laughter was an out-pouring of their joy. The children were a boy of five, another of four, and a two-year-old girl. A year and a half ago, they had been victims of child abuse at the hands of their drug-addicted parents. Now they were in jail with many years left in the state penitentiary for violating their children's trust with blows and other signs of physical abuse. But on this particular day, a couple in their fifties walked into the courtroom following the children. Their tanned faces belied years of toiling under the hot desert sun in the agricultural fields. When they all sat before the judge, the children hopped up on the laps of the couple that beginning today, would become their adoptive parents. The four-year-old pulled on the cheeks of his soon to be dad, while trying to comb his graying hair with his hands. The girl was leaning on her soon to be mom who was fixing the curls on the girl's forehead. The five-year-old was waving "hi" to the judge who was taking his seat on the stand. The formalities were brief. The parents signed the adoption documents, and then the judge read out loud the oath of adoption. "The adoptive children will have all the rights and privileges of children as if they had been born to you, including the right of inheritance. The new names of the children will be . . ." As the judge read the children's name, they giggled as they heard their names spoken by such an important looking man. None of the children really had any idea of what just happened. But their future was now assured by the love of their new parents. As soon as the ceremony was over, the judge invited the new family to join him in the judge's stand to have their picture taken with him. The four-year-old held the gavel in his hands.

The Scriptures testify that God sent Jesus "to buy freedom for us who were slaves to the law, so that he could adopt us as his very own children. And because we are his children, God has sent the Spirit of his Son into our hearts, prompting us to call out, 'Abba, Father.' Now you are no longer a slave but God's own child. And since you are his child, God has made you his heir" (Galatians 4:5-7 NLT). On the cross, Jesus Christ embraced us as His own children. He paid the ultimate price for our adoption, without even asking us if we wanted to be His children. Just as those children in the courtroom were totally unaware of their adoptive parents' oath to benefit them, so we were totally unaware that on the cross He was securing our eternal future. When He died for our sins and rose on the third day, Jesus Christ signed with His own blood the certificate of our adoption. Thus, He became the Guarantor of our future, eternally loved by Him as His own children. Through Him we are heirs of everything there is in the universe, and forever! And to think that at times we have thought we were worth nothing! We are even given the faith to believe it! Confess it in your heart that you have a new Dad and Mom, a new home, a new family that will always love you and will never abandon you throughout eternity. Without you even asking for it, or knowing it. It was already yours when you were born. That gift is entirely yours by faith alone, even if it is just the tiniest atomic particle of faith. For those who find it difficult to believe, faith is given in just that microscopic quantum size. Let your heart feel the embrace of your heavenly Father, and your new brothers and sisters throughout the world and the universe. And yes, He says to call Him, "Daddy!"

11

I Want My Marriage Annulled

> The Lord appeared to me in a faraway place and said, "I love you with an everlasting love. So I will continue to show you my kindness . . . Christ also loved the church and gave Himself for it . . . that He might present to Himself a glorious church, not having spot, or wrinkle, or any such thing, but that it should be holy and without blemish . . . This is a great mystery, but I am speaking about Christ and the church" (Jeremiah 31:3 GW; Ephesians 5:25-27, 32 NIV).

A gentleman in his forties came before the judge requesting the annulment of his marriage. "Please state the reason," said the judge rather coolly.

"I wasn't quite in all my five senses when I got married," answered the petitioner.

"Hardly anyone is ever in their senses when they get married," joked the judge. "Why is your insanity any different?"

"Well, Your Honor, that happened nearly twenty-two years ago. "We'd gone to Las Vegas with a group of friends to celebrate someone's eighteenth birthday. Once there, we met up with some girls. I hit it off just right with one of them. We all partied and got drunk. One of her girlfriends joked that since we were getting on so well, we should call a clown to marry us. Ha, ha. Everyone liked the idea. Soon after, the clown showed up, also drunk, and as if it were one great big joke, he crossed himself and had us genuflect, said some kind of blessing, and declared us husband and wife. The clown charged us a bottle of whisky, took our names down "just to show the boss," and we all fell asleep drunk, all over the hotel room. The girl woke up and left before I did, and I never saw her again. For me, it had all been a joke."

"Quite an expensive joke," retorted the judge.

But the petitioner continued, "Thing is, now I do want to get married. But when I went to the county clerk, to my surprise, the record showed that I'd been married all these years! The clown had not been jesting, no joke! The clown had given our personal information to the clerk, and I had been registered as married!"

Since sometimes the obvious needs to be said, marriage is no joking matter, and it's clear that what happens in Vegas, doesn't always stay in Vegas. But eons ago there was another marriage sealed by the heavenly Judge. Jesus Christ, the Sovereign King and Creator of the universe took His marriage vows to become one with the humanity of our planet. He vowed to marry this rebellious planet, full of unbelieving, perverse, blaspheming, unhinged, and crime-ridden people, bent on destroying their own earthly home. There has never been such a mismatched couple. We (the wife) have thought that story is nothing but a fairy tale, a romantic lunacy. We have turned our backs on our Groom, and given ourselves over to one great orgy of drunkenness, addictions without number, out of control greed and envy. Our Husband's response? Faithfulness. Unwavering commitment. "I have loved you with an everlasting love; I have drawn you with unfailing kindness . . . How long will you wander, unfaithful Daughter Israel? The Lord will create a new thing on earth—the woman will return to the man" (Jeremiah 31:3,22 NIV). The eternal lover seeks to win His lover's heart with an ultimate sacrifice, called upon by His love. That's what Jesus Christ did on the cross. There, He took upon Himself all the guilt and sin of earth's inhabitants, and to get rid of their inherent condemnation, He died for each one of them. That great love leaves us with mouth agape, speechless, and pulls us toward Him. It's in the eternal forecast; the word has been given, "the woman will return to the man."

"Christ loved the church and gave himself up for her . . . to present her to himself as a radiant church, without stain or wrinkle or any other blemish, but holy and blameless . . . This is a profound mystery—but I am talking about Christ and the church" (Ephesians 5:25-27, 31-32 NIV). Look at the scars on His hands. With those hands, He signed the marriage certificate. That indeed is no joke. We've belonged to Him since eons ago. And He will never abandon us. It's a marriage never to be annulled!

12

A Painful Sentence

> "For Christ also has once suffered for sins, the just for the unjust, so that He might bring us to God . . . Therefore, there is now no condemnation for those who are in Christ Jesus" (1 Peter 3:18 NET; Romans 8:1 NIV).

That afternoon, a twenty-five-year-old man would be sentenced to twenty-five years in prison. I was there to translate the sentencing. As I approached him, our eyes met briefly. What I saw in those eyes was anguish, desperation. It seemed as if his soul was crying out loud. His defense attorney coolly asked me to let him know that he would be sentenced to twenty-five years in prison. As I translated the words, his eyes immediately became moist and red, and his eyelids began to tremble. He lowered his head under the weight of the sentence. The judge read it out loud. As I translated, I tried to drown out from my own soul this young man's personal drama. How do you tell someone that he will spend the rest of his youth in jail? It's during those years when a person has the opportunity to get an education, marry the woman of his dreams, experience the joy of holding his first baby in his arms, practice his favorite sport, enjoy his parents and grandparents. This young man would lose all that. I asked him if he had family in the courtroom. Making a gesture with his lips he pointed to a young woman. I immediately noticed her. Her face was pale. But her face did not reflect pity but a deep anger. This young man, her boyfriend, for a period of four years had been sexually abusing her nieces. At least four lives had been terribly hurt. The young teens who had lost their childhood innocence, the young man who was giving up his future to the uncertain fortune of the state penitentiary, and the young woman who was overwhelmed by so many conflicting emotions. She felt betrayal, pity, anger, and the loss of her most beautiful and pure hopes: having a home and family with a young man who she once had dared to love. I felt pained by the sentence that would most likely drown him in all the moral filth of prison, but there's no doubt that's the least he deserved!

But what does God feel about our sentence? Scripture says, "I take no pleasure in the death of the wicked" (Ezekiel 33:11 NIV). It doesn't matter if we consider our sins "just small stuff" compared to the evil perversions of pedophiles. Before God, every offense, no matter how small, is an offense against His law of love, and that same law condemns us to spend eternity separated from God, to the misery of living devoid of love and being loved. God feels infinite pain at seeing us condemned to that miserable sentence. Indeed we were condemned but in the body of His Son in whom He is well pleased. What must have been the heart wrenching pain of that decision is beyond our comprehension. But that is what it took to keep us from living out that sentence of living and dying without Him. "For Christ also died for sins once for all, the righteous for the unrighteous, that he might bring us to God" (1 Peter 3:18 NASB). God our Father sacrificed Himself so that there would be only one sacrifice, the willing sacrifice of His Son, instead of billions of human beings abandoned throughout eternity to the worst prison imaginable: to live and die without hope and love, kept company only by our remorse. "There is therefore now no more condemnation for those who are in Christ Jesus" (Romans 8:1 NIV). At the moment when the eternal Judge pronounces your sentence, Jesus intervenes, and He receives it on your behalf. And that already took place on the cross. Why? Because He loves you, and God, who is life and love in Himself, cannot live without you. This love is for you and me. It is ours only to receive it by faith alone, no matter how many voices cry out against you to the contrary.

13

Identity Theft: "Who Done It?"

> "But he was wounded for the wrong we did; he was crushed
> for the evil we did. The punishment, which made us well,
> was given to him, and we are healed because of his wounds"
> (Isaiah 53:5 EXB).

One of the crimes that causes the greatest personal outrage is identity theft. But it's not merely theft manipulating bank accounts with computers or stealing credit cards. There's another type of identity theft that's simpler, yet more perverse. When the police stop a suspect, let's say for drunk driving, he does not give his true identity. Since he's also driving without a license, the suspect gives another name, that of a relative, close in age and appearance. The police then issue him a summons to appear in court. In it, he's ordered to show up in court for arraignment on the charge of drunk driving and related charges. On that day, of course, the suspect who was stopped does not appear in court. It's you who were supposed to appear in court, but you don't have the slightest idea why. You were busy at work. You are totally unaware of a summons in your name and the charges against you. You are totally blind to everything that's going on behind the scenes that will soon surprise you.

Since you didn't appear in court, the judge issues an arrest warrant. The police have your address since they find your name in the Department of Motor Vehicles data bank. Sooner rather than later, the police show up at your home. If you're lucky, they will just give you another summons. But most likely, the police will arrest you since

now you have another pending charge: failure to appear. As the officer tucks your head into the patrol car, you are in total shock, angry,
helpless. The more you appeal and complain to the police that they
are making a mistake, the more they insist, "That's what we hear all
the time. Can you come up with a new one?"

If you're able, you post bail. You go home with a new court date,
still scratching your head as to what happened. You've never driven
under the influence; your driving record is totally clean. Someone
posed as you, and you were charged with several crimes and infractions. But you know you are innocent, yet you don't know who is to
blame, the one who is really guilty of the crimes. When you eventually
make the court appearance and are given a public defender, she, of
course, does not let you plead guilty. She requests an investigation. In
time, the investigation reveals that it was one of your own relatives,
a cousin, brother, sister who committed the crime, and for their own
convenience posed as you! This type of identity theft tears apart family relationships, instigates all kinds of hatred and mistrust between
people who once loved and respected each other. There's no end to
the clashes, feuds, blaming and counter blaming, because in the end,
someone had to pay the fines!

Scripture affirms that indeed there was someone who took our
identity, but it was all for our good. In His life, and on the cross, Jesus
assumed our identity, not as guiltless, but our identity as sinners, guilty
of being nothing but evil. However, Jesus took on our identity and in
our place received the just condemnation of the law. But Scripture
also affirms that it was our identity as evil sinners that He assumed.
"God made him who had no sin to be sin for us, so that in him we
might become the righteousness of God" (2 Corinthains 5:21 NIV).
Before God, Jesus exchanged His identity with us. He took our identity as sinners on Himself, and bestowed on us His identity as the
righteous, pure, loving, and holy one of God, altogether apart from
any merit from us or in us, or worked out by us. Thus, when we are
called before the judgment seat of God, He declares us righteous,
altogether guiltless, worthy of eternal life! Not because of who we are,
but because of who He is.

The identity thief of our story took someone's identity without
the other person knowing, at a moment in time totally unknown to
the real person. In an ironic twist, Jesus also took our identity without

our knowledge; I was totally unaware. In fact, it was done before I was even born. It was a *fait accompli* at the cross, over 2,000 years ago! My sinner identity was taken from me at the cross. I wasn't even consulted. Good thing because I would have certainly been offended. I would have objected, reclaimed it, and snatched it back!

14

When The Teddy Bears Wept

> "Having predestined us for adoption as children through Jesus Christ to himself, according to the good pleasure of his desire" (Ephesians 1:5 NHEB).

The courtroom was ready. It had been decorated with hanging cotton clouds, figures of parrots, owls, lions, giraffes, racing cars, sailboats, little airplanes of all types, and sparkly ribbons. There were also all kinds of stuffed animals ready for the new adoptees: a huge panda bear, a tiger with squiggly large stripes, a monkey hanging by its tail from one of the windows, and a huge Orca whale with black and white stripes. There was a beautifully decorated chocolate cake with pink and blue colors and animal designs set on the attorney's table. The court was waiting for three boys and a girl, ages twelve, ten, nine, and seven respectively. The judge was pacing nervously in the hallway just outside the courtroom, and was already wearing his judicial robe. The attorneys nervously peered out the windows to the parking lot. The courtroom clerk picked up the phone receiver several times while dialing different numbers. One could sense the tension over the family's delay. Finally, she motioned to the Adoption Department attorney to pick up on the other phone. I was there to translate for the proceedings since the children did not speak English well. We could only hear what the attorney was saying. "Say what? You can't make it today? What happened? Don't you have transportation? We can send a vehicle to pick you up. No? Is one of the kids sick? No? Then, why can't you make it? What? Please say that again; I didn't understand. You are going to what?

The attorneys and the judge were already around the phone trying to listen. At that moment, the attorney pressed the speaker function on the phone so that all could hear. The man's voice on the other end was loud and clear, "It's that my wife and I are getting a divorce." There was a click, and then, the dull sound of the dial tone. We all looked at each other in disbelief, frustration, and disappointment. Everyone had something to say.

"They were such a good couple for those kids." "How come that didn't show up in the investigation?" "I wonder if there's something we can do." "Where are the kids now?" "We better send the police to pick up the kids and place them in another foster home." Then the courtroom went quiet again. Everyone was looking up at the teddy bears and monkeys hanging from the ceiling. Then down at the cake. Without talking any more about what we'd do next, we all found a chair and kept not one, but several minutes of silence. Finally, the judge broke the silence, addressing the court clerk. "The matter is off calendar."

What if Jesus hadn't shown up for us at the cross for our adoption? What if the entire human race would have been left waiting at the foot of an empty cross for its redeemer? What if a prophet would have appeared on Mount Calvary crying out, "He's not coming, He can't make it, He changed His mind, things got too complicated for Him! There's been a disagreement in the Trinity. The Son wants to adopt sinners by grace alone; the Father and the Spirit want conditions. They could not come to an agreement. Too bad. Everyone is left to their own misery, sin, and condemnation. The promise of the Seed that would bless all nations won't be fulfilled. There won't be any justification, or eternal life. No forgiveness of sins by grace through faith. The Law is there already. Do the best you can with that. Some might make it, no guarantee though. You are your own redeemers, your own Messiahs. Use Scriptures to get all the power you can to meet the requirements of perfection. It won't happen any other way. Isaiah 53 was a major blunder in inspiration. It's not going to happen like that. The Seed won't be wounded for your transgressions. He won't be pierced for your transgressions; He won't be crushed for your iniquities. It was all a major divine *faux pas*. There won't be a cry of "it is finished"; you'll have to finish it on your own. There won't be a burial either. You'll have to die to your sin all by yourself, just do your best when death overtakes you. Try your hardest to resurrect on the third day, just claim the power to do it, see if that works. And if you do it, then hope you can make the long jump to the presence of God, and stand there blameless before God. See if your righteousness will be accepted. Wash your hands really well; they've got to be clean. And your heart, altogether pure, not even the tiniest spot of sin . . ." And so on. Prophets like these never run out of good advice.

But He did show up. That's the testimony of Scripture. "But when the set time had fully come, God sent his Son, born of a woman, born under the law, to redeem those under the law, that we might receive adoption to sonship" (Galatians 4:4-5 NIV). "The time is fulfilled, and the kingdom of God is at hand; repent, and believe in the gospel" (Mark 1:14 NASB). "Having predestined us for adoption as children through Jesus Christ to himself, according to the good pleasure of his desire" (Ephesians 1:5 NHEB). At the cross He signed our certificate of adoption, without presenting us with a list of preconditions, or any conditions at all. He had met all the conditions; He finished the entire adoption process on His own. He declared us to be His adopted children, forever. He would not go back on His word, for His word is the word of the Father and the Spirit. And they all say, "come." By faith we've been already ushered into the divine courtroom, not to be adopted, but to be given our certificate of adoption, with our own new names, and then to enjoy the party. No empty banquet table there. Our entire family in heaven and on earth will be there. No stuffed teddy bears there, neither light, sun, moon, or stars, for the Lamb Himself will be our eternal refuge, and His leaves, the leaves from the tree of life, His cross, will be for our healing, and the healing of the nations.

15

The Seal Can't Be Broken

> They took up a new song, saying, "You are worthy to take the scroll and open its seals, because you were slain, and by your blood you purchased for God persons from every tribe, language, people, and nation . . . Blessing, honor, glory, and power belong to the one seated on the throne and to the Lamb forever and always" (Revelation 5:9,13 CEB).

The public defender stood beside his client as they both faced the judge. The attorney was presenting a plea to break the seal of a document containing accusatory evidence. It was the original Arrest Warrant. Months before, the police with warrant in hand had searched the business and several properties of the accused. In one of her rentals, several boxes were found containing heroin, cocaine, and other party drugs packaged and ready for shipment. Similar merchandise was found at a business registered in her name. Therefore, the District Attorney was charging her with transport and sales of narcotics. They were serious charges punishable by many years in the state penitentiary if convicted. But who had snitched on her? Who had accused her? Who had exposed her? Who had actually called the police? Who knew what? Her defense attorney needed that information to prepare her defense. But all those documents were sealed, allegedly for the security and safety of the informants. The seal on the evidence folder meant that all the witnesses were very close to the defendant, and it was they who had denounced her.

As it turned out, one of the accusers had criminal charges pending, but had cut a deal with the District Attorney to appear as a witness at her trial in exchange for a more lenient jail sentence. But now, her defense attorney was pleading with the judge to unseal the evidence folder. That's precisely the information the attorney suspected was there. He believed that the secrecy was not so much to protect the witnesses, but to cover the deal one of the accusers had cut with the District Attorney. Thus, he rightfully claimed that it was impossible to defend her client's rights without access to those records.

The judge answered that he needed some time to look over the initial pleadings from the District Attorney to see if it was within the purview of the law to break the seal. The proceedings went into a short recess while the judge studied the pleadings. A few minutes later, the session reconvened to hear the judge's ruling: "I can't break the seal. It contains very sensitive information. It is reserved solely and strictly for the upcoming trial. The final ruling will be given then with respect to the unsealing of the evidence."

The Scriptures speak of a certain scroll, which was also sealed. "Then I saw in the right hand of him who sat on the throne a scroll with writing on both sides and sealed with seven seals. And I saw a mighty angel proclaiming in a loud voice, "Who is worthy to break the seals and open the scroll?" But no one in heaven or on earth or under the earth could open the scroll or even look inside it. I wept and wept because no one was found who was worthy to open the scroll or look inside" (Revelation 5:1-4 NIV). The scroll contains the name of everyone who has ever lived, lives today, and will ever live on the surface of this planet. So, our name is also written there, with everything that identifies us, like let's say our DNA code. There are no duplicate names on the scroll. Everyone is unique, everyone with their unique composition, time of birth and death is found there. Our name also contains all our family and personal history, our moral and ethical history, all our work and leisure history, all the apparent good we've done with its respective motivations, all our failures with their respective pretexts and justifications, plus much more than we don't even know about ourselves. And let us not forget all our good and evil intentions, which we've never carried out in life, but quite so in our imaginations. All our hostile and angry thoughts against every possible person that has ever crossed us, even those very dear to us.

But this scroll also contains the names of the forgiven. It is the most important document that has ever existed in the entire universe. It is the writ we would most like to see, and dread the most if it were shown to us. The apostle John cried without comfort when he saw this scroll was sealed, and even more when no one could open it. All those before the heavenly court plead for the scroll to be opened, but there was no one worthy, no one morally, ethically, or spiritually qualified for the task. Finally, a cry was heard directed at Jesus Christ, the Lamb of God: "You are worthy to take the scroll and to open its seals, because you were slain, and with your blood you purchased for God persons from every tribe and language and people and nation" (Revelation 5:9 NIV).

There was no hesitation, protest, or opposition from the heavenly judge. At the sound of Jesus's name, the Father extends the scroll and Jesus's hands receive it from the Father. The Father doesn't need a further examination of the scroll, or a questioning of the Son to determine His qualifications to open it. The scars in the hands of the Son are His qualifications. No one dare oppose Him. The Son deliberately tears open the seals, and the names of the forgiven flash from the scroll in one great beam of light. Your name is there. So is mine. Gone are all our personal histories. Gone is all the sensitive, delicate, and damning information. There are no accusers; every single piece of evidence disappears from our record. Only one history stands in its place: the history of the life, death, and resurrection of the Lamb. The perfect record of Him who is called "The Holy One of God." And the magnificent heavenly choir breaks forth in the grandest choral harmony: "To him who sits on the throne and to the Lamb be praise and honor and glory and power, for ever and ever!" (Revelation 5:13 NIV). You and I are free to live and love, and love forever!

16

I Just Didn't Think Twice About It

> "For the wages of sin is death, but the gift of God is eternal life in Christ Jesus, our Lord . . . But God shows his love for us, because while we were still sinners Christ died for us" (Romans 6:23, 5:28 ESV).

She was already wringing her hands as she walked into the courtroom. It wasn't cold. It was obvious she was just nervous. Once I interpreted the judge's initial instructions, she asked me if I thought she'd get locked up today. I refrained from sharing my suspicions. When the judge called her name, she stood up wiping tears, attempting to maintain her composure. The judge read the charges against her. "Breaking and entry with intention to commit a felony, theft, attempt to cash checks with false identification, unauthorized use of credit cards, attempting to defraud a banking institution." They were all felonies, each charge punishable by three years in the state penitentiary if convicted. A total of a fifteen-year prison term. The judge granted her the services of a public defender, and shortly after, we proceeded to the interview room. "What happened? It's that I'm a single mother; I've got three girls, five, three, and a one-year-old. I clean houses to support them and my aging grandparents. I was dusting the lady's dresser when I saw those signed checks sitting there. I thought about the meds my youngest girl needed, and then I just didn't think twice about it . . . But now, they're going to lock me up and take my girls away from me . . ." Her tears, cries, and sighs stifled her words.

The public defender just told her, "I'm going to have a word with the judge. Just sit back in the courtroom and wait 'till I call you back here." A while later we went back to the interview room where I interpreted the attorney's good news. "The judge is going to drop three of the five charges. Then, if you just plead guilty to one, he'll give you ninety days of community service, and three years' probation. You'll get to keep your girls. This is your first offense, and it must be your last.

Crying once again, but now for joy, through sobs and tears, she accepted the judge's offer. Yes, I was just as surprised as you are now. It was too lenient a sentence. She wasn't even ordered restitution payments. Of course, the bank had caught the attempted fraud, so the owner of the checks wasn't out any money. Still, the sentence seemed too lax compared to how other defendants had been treated for less serious charges. But this judge was known for his occasional good mood days. The single mother had lucked out; she happened to show up on one of those. Or, had it been just a sob story that had touched the judge's heart on one of his better moods? But he wasn't known for buying "poor me" stories.

But before the heavenly court, no one gets a break depending on the Judge's mood or anyone's sob story. Every sin receives the same sentence, and the worst: "For the wages of sin is death" (Romans 6:23). The sentence is not based on the judge's good or bad moods. Everyone pays the same death sentence, but in the body of another, the body of a substitute, provided by the God of love. That other is Jesus the Christ, very God of very God, who took human form and stands in for us before God in all things, including our sin, sentencing, and life before God. A complete and full judicial gift in one Person, given unconditionally by grace through faith alone. He alone received the sentence. He died, but that we may live before God. "But the gift of God is eternal life in Jesus Christ, our Lord" (Romans 6:23 ESV). It is already a done deal, a historical fact that cannot be erased by our attempts to re-write history "sharing how we helped out." Our history was substituted by the history of Christ, on a cross on Mount Calvary, two thousand years ago. We died, were buried, and rose again to eternal life in those three brief days. That is the good news that nullifies all hand wringing, wipes away every tear, from every eye. It's not that the charges are dropped based on the judge's good humor. It's the Other's living, dying, and arising again in His own person, on behalf of everyone who has ever had human DNA on the face of this planet. Even those who have done the most perverse, heinous, and evil things to others? Yes. Even those who have done such a perverse thing as asking that question, for they have installed themselves as gods and questioned the Father's generosity with the riches of His grace. But what about those who have only done good things and bring them as offerings before God? The Lord will say to them, "Depart from me, for you do nothing but evil things" (Matthew 7:23 AMPC). All their pious and religious lifestyle is declared to be nothing but evil! But why? Because they have put aside the perfect life and sacrifice of the Substitute and dare approach the eternal Judge on their own limited terms. Yes, they bring a long list of love-motivated impressive tasks done for others. But they could have done so much more! They could have loved ever more sincerely! They could have sacrificed so much more! They could have fed so many more hungry people, clothed so many more naked, visited so many more people in jail! And yet they persist in thinking that there is plenty of intrinsic value in those works. "We've done them in faith and love, we've done them sincerely, we've done them in your name," they insist.

They pass perfect judgment on themselves, as if they were God, declaring their meager works of self-interest as acceptable and sufficient! Such is the magnitude of God's holiness that it declares all human goodness as inherent evil and worthy of condemnation. But what about those like the slick-handed housekeeper of our story who just couldn't help herself? What about those with little self-control? Those who just on a whim showed up for work at 5:00 p.m. because they had been sinning all day long? Oh, those? They go to the front of the line first, because Christ's impulse to save is greater than their impulse to sin!

Because of Christ, and only because of Him, God delights in showing mercy to all, pardoning iniquity and justifying the wicked. There's no hand wringing when our name is called. Instead, all are called to come with open hands to receive faith and salvation through the infinite gift of His perfect life. For "God shows his love for us in that while we were yet sinners Christ died for us" (Romans 5:8 ESV). No sob story needed to win His love. No moody God that will save on His good days but condemn on others. Because of Christ, it is His nature to seek and save the lost, and save them to the uttermost!

17

We Didn't Know What Was In The Back Pack

> "I advise you to buy from me gold made pure in fire so you can be truly rich. Buy from me white clothes so you can be clothed and so you can cover your shameful nakedness. Buy from me medicine to put on your eyes so you can truly see . . . On the day when I act in judgment, they will be my own special treasure. I will spare them as a father spares an obedient child" (Revelation 3:18 NCV: Malachi 3:17 NLT).

So, they married and lived happily ever after? We'll never know. This playful couple was living it up one night at a nightclub in a nearby city. They downed some salty-sweet, lemon rim margaritas to add more fun to their dancing away the night. There was laughter and unchecked excitement. As they danced, they were the center of attention. Applause and more drinks. Things went on until a well-dressed gentleman approached them. He offered them a deal. By mistake, he'd forgotten a backpack that belonged to a friend in a city some 160 kilometers away. Driving time was less than two hours along the four-lane freeway. He offered them $600.00 (six hundred dollars) "for their trouble." There they were: six one hundred-dollar bills in his hand reached out to them. Of course, they needed the money. Besides, they had already spent way too much at the club. With the bills, they could make up for what they'd "blown away" that night. "Let's do it; it's already past midnight. We live in that town anyway." They took the backpack, plunked it in the trunk of their car, and off they went.

But with the margaritas working away at their neurons, the young driver's foot on the pedal was heavier than usual, and he swerved more than he should have as he went from lane to lane, passing the late-night traffic. His girlfriend cheered him on. A highway patrol was on an off-ramp monitoring traffic, and after a brief chase, pulled them over. The young driver was asked to blow into the Breathalyzer, and the result showed alcohol content three times the legal limit. Following her instincts, the patrolwoman asked the couple to exit the vehicle for the required search in an alcohol stop. There in the backseat was the backpack. She asked them if they knew what was in it. They told her the story, just doing it for a friend, didn't know a thing. Inside the backpack were eighteen kilos of drugs (almost forty lbs.)! Cocaine, methamphetamines, ecstasy, marijuana, with a street value of $600,000.00 USD (six-hundred thousand dollars)!

Days later, they found themselves in the courtroom and needing an interpreter. I was there to translate for the arraignment. They were both twenty-years-old. They listened as the defense attorney interviewed them before the judge called their names. "It's quite serious," was the attorney's understatement. "Each one of you is facing up to thirty years in jail. The charges are illegal transport and trafficking of narcotics with intention to sell, enhanced by the large quantity of drugs. Each drug carries its own separate charge. Can you explain to me what you were doing with that backpack? What's going to be your defense?"

Without hesitation, both answered at the same time and with the same words: "It's that we didn't know what was in the backpack!"

The attorney's response was mock astonishment: "Really?"

They had listened to a lie, in a place where lies are the number one product for sale, for all that apparent joy and laughter is but a large transparent bubble. Even their alibi seemed preposterous! But everything seemed real. Even a serendipitous encounter. The offer seemed more than a coincidence, perhaps a blessing, that with only a two-hour trip, they could pay their rent for one month, plus pay for their spree at the club. Such is the father of lies. Fools' gold instead of real bullions, straw instead of silver. Prison instead of freedom. These are the offers from that enemy of our souls dressed up as a fine gentleman offering the deal of our lives. But it's just a curse instead of a blessing. He camouflages the curse as a blessing and dresses up blessings as curses. And we all, in one way or another, have fallen for the decoys and slipped into his traps. That is why the divine Judge tells us, "Therefore I counsel you to buy from me gold refined by fire, that you may be rich, and white garments to clothe you and to keep the shame of your nakedness from being seen, and salve to anoint your eyes, that you may see" (Revelation 3:18 NIV). All of these riches do not come in a backpack of dubious content. Instead, they come wrapped up in one person: Jesus, the Christ. He is our gold. He is our pure garment. He is our healing. He is our sanity. He is our wholeness. He is our integrity. He is the substitute for our addictions. He is our life and freedom. He is our righteousness before God. He is the pearl of great price that adorns our lives. All these riches in the perfect wrapping of His person is ours by grace alone, through faith alone, to His glory alone. Everything else is slavery and prison bars. But on the cross, he broke down the prison bars and cried out, 'you are mine, you are my special possession as I take your sin upon this cross, and I will spare you as a man spares his children who serve him' (Malachi 3:17 NRSV).

Thus, in our interview with our Attorney, we can only say, "Yes, we knew all along what was in the backpack. We took it from Adam, who took it from "the serpent who was more subtle than any other creature." Each generation has gotten the backpack hand off and added its own junk as well, until as a huge ball and chain, it holds the entire creation captive to its condemnation. But on the cross, the Christ took the chain off our feet and nailed it to his own that we might go free into the kingdom of his life, where there are no lies. There are only truths; in fact, there's only one truth, the truth that saves, sets free, and lifts the offending backpack. For God so loved the partying, condemned world, that he gave his only son that whoever believes in him, should not be held under the power and weight of sin, but be set free. And in that freedom, they enter into the ecstatic joy of him who loved us and made us a kingdom and priests to God his Father—to him be the glory and the power forever. Amen. (Revelation 1:6 NIV).

18

Released From Double Jeopardy

> "If you confess with your mouth that Jesus is Lord and believe in your heart that God raised him from the dead, you will be saved. For with the heart one believes and is justified, and with the mouth one confesses and is saved. For the Scripture says, 'Everyone who believes in him will not be put to shame'" (Romans 10:9-10 ESV).

The public defender advised the defendant: "If you plead guilty now, before your trial is over, you'll only get three years jail time. But since you've already been locked up nearly three years awaiting trial, you'll most likely be freed in just a few weeks. You'll be given credit for time served. Sure, you'll be deported when you're released, but you'll be free in your own country. There will be a long jail sentence waiting for you if come back. But, if you *don't* take the offer, you'll most likely be found guilty and sentenced. The charges are extremely serious. Rape of a minor, and on repeated occasions. If the jury finds you guilty, you'll most likely be given a life sentence. If you take the deal, you'll be sure of your sentence, and you'll be released soon. However, if you continue to claim your right to trial, you'll most likely lose your freedom forever, and you'll never go back to your family, your kids, your job, and your friends. You'll be locked up forever without the possibility of parole."

But the defendant insisted on his innocence, even as the attorney reminded him of the risk. "It's almost a foregone conclusion that the jury will find you guilty of all thirty counts of rape against your stepdaughter, throughout a two-year period, beginning when she was eleven-years-old until your arrest a day after her thirteenth birthday." But the man claimed the minor's mother had enlisted the stepdaughter to make the false accusations because he refused to increase monthly child and spousal support payments in what had been a nasty divorce. The alleged evidence was basically the minor's word against his, and the minor had stated she would testify at trial. She was already a teenager in high school, and was the next witness scheduled to appear on the witness stand.

The attorney continued. "This jury is nearly all women, and they will most likely believe her and not you."

As I translated, I could hear the man mouth to himself his inner struggle, "Do I plead guilty to charges I did not commit and go free? Or, do I insist on my innocence but risk the life sentence?"

Our dilemma before God is worse than this defendant's. At least his jail time awaiting trial counted as "credit for time served." He'd be let go after three years. His "locked up" time at least gave him the option for an early release. But our time "dead in our sins and trespasses" amounts to nothing. In fact, it's the opposite. It's actually "debit for time served." Because we have been living in the prison of our sinful nature, that very fact testifies of our guilt and deserved condemnation. We pay for nothing with our life of sin. All our self-inflicted pain is worthless, totally futile. So, God offers no deal for our "time served." Sin is time served in vain. Further, we can't fool ourselves into thinking we can work out a deal with God, because prisoners have no choice. Our guilty plea is also fatally flawed. Our admissions of guilt before God always have at their nucleus nothing but swirling pretexts and justifications. They are also wrapped up in fear of punishment, to say nothing of self-interest. They are imperfect guilty pleas. God reads right through their hypocrisy. We have nothing over the pedophile of our story. His guilty plea was his ticket to freedom. Not much remorse there.

Going to trial before God is even more futile, yet inevitable, "For we must all appear before the judgment seat of Christ, so that each one may receive good or evil, according to what he has done in the body" (1 Corinthians 5:10 RSV). But we also know from Scripture that no one will receive the good. All will receive evil, "since all have sinned and continue to fall short of God's glory" and "the wages of sin is death." It is a trial where we all know where the verdict and the sentencing will land. Except that our Attorney, Jesus Christ steps in. He does not advise us to plead guilty. We already saw the intrinsic flaws of our guilty pleas. But He will do the unthinkable. He will plead guilty on our behalf and suffer the death sentence in our place. His guilty plea is the only sincere and thoroughly heartfelt admission of guilt there has ever been. His strategy is trustworthy. It's infallible. We just sit back in jail, believe in His already finished work, and the jail doors will bust open. In fact, He presides over the biggest jail bust in history. And there is a dramatic, unexpected twist. As the jail doors burst open and we are set free, the devil and all his minions are locked up. The evil one can do absolutely nothing as he watches us run free, celebrating our freedom. He will not be the next witness to take the stand against us. His days as "the accuser of the brothers and sisters" are all over (Revelation 12:10 NIV). His accusations and cries are not heard outside his prison cell. If he were indeed to take the witness stand against us, the father of lies would tell the sordid truth about us, but embellished with his own slandering genius. However, we have nothing to fear.

Our only plea before God is the one that Christ entered on our behalf. It is recorded as a plea of David, but proleptically, it is Christ's own plea on the cross when he took our sins on his guiltless soul: "Do not enter into judgment with your slave for before you no human being will be justified" (Psalm 143:2 KJV). And yet, through this desperate cry, admitting guilt on behalf of all sinners, we are all declared entirely righteous, pure, and loving, as though we had never offended anyone with our deeds, hurt ourselves with our thoughts, or failed to care for God's creation.

As we leave the heavenly courtroom, our song, together with the countless throng of the redeemed, will be, "We have been justified by his grace as a gift, through the redemption which is in Christ Jesus" (Romans 3:24 ESV). "To him who sits on the throne and to the Lamb be praise and honor and glory and power, for ever and ever!" (Revelation 5:13 GW).

19

Sputum Dictum

> "I glorified you on earth, having accomplished the work that you gave me to do ... "Father, if you are willing, remove this cup from me. Nevertheless, not my will, but yours, be done" (John 17:4 ESV; Luke 22:42 ESV).

There are courtroom dramas that are barely seen or heard. On this occasion, the protagonists were a father and his son. The son was detained. He had been brought from jail to the detainee's box. Today was just one of many delayed hearings for his preliminary hearing. He was facing various serious charges: drug possession, breaking and entry of a business, theft, and other related misdemeanors. The young man, barely out of his teens, was quite a spectacle. His entire face was covered with tattoos, as well as his arms, clear down to his fingertips. His gaze was threatening with more than a touch of insolence.

Sitting in the crowded courtroom was a gentleman in his sixties. His face and arms had other markings. The wrinkles of age and the unmistakable tan of having worked for many years under the scorching sun in the agricultural fields. His gaze displayed a sober mixture of sad anxiety. As I interpreted to the young man the various nuances of the charges against him, he seemed more interested in cleaning his fingernails than in my translation of the attorney's instructions. As soon as the attorney finished, the defendant spoke to him, "Tell my f***ing dad to put some coins in my jail account . . . I ran out . . . and tell him I wanna talk to him on the phone."

Minutes later we were out in the hallway, delivering the message to the father. As we spoke to him, tears welled up in his reddening eyes, "Sure, but please tell him not to yell and curse at me."

We went back to his son and gave him the message. His reaction? With the same insolent gaze, he searched out his dad in the courtroom. When their eyes met, he hurled a mouthed obscenity in his dad's direction and faked a spat to the courtroom floor. The father reeled back as if shot by a bullet. He then leaned forward, lowered his gaze, put on his cap, and head lowered, walked out of the courtroom. I could see his shoulders trembling from his muffled cries.

Every fiber of our being reels at this kind of behavior toward any parent. But we're not far from doing the same. Sometimes we catch ourselves murmuring criticism under our breath about our aging parents, perhaps even mocking them as we did when we were kids, or quickly denying what may seem to us as a totally unnecessary request. But the Ancient of Days in his heavenly throne leaves us without excuse: "Honor your father and your mother" (Exodus 20:12 ESV). If we don't honor sincerely from our hearts, the words that come out of our mouths are mere nonsense, and our parents know it. In fact, anyone knows whether we are sincere in our compliments, or whether there's a degree of self-interest attached to our "honor." We have all failed in our "honoring" of the other, especially those with whom we have serious differences of any kind. There's only One who has perfectly honored His Father. He lovingly kept and fulfilled His Father's will, which was beyond any imaginable task our parents ever thought of giving us. "I glorified you on earth by finishing the work that you gave me to do" (John 17:4 EHV). "I have come . . . to do your will, O God" (Hebrews 10:7 NCB). He fulfilled the most difficult task anyone has ever had to accomplish: taking on his sinless body our horrible and most perverse sins. With just one of our sins, he would already have had enough reason to plead before the Father to modify the task. But when he drank that bitter cup filled with the filthiness of our evil, he was honoring the Father saying, "Father, if you are willing, remove this cup from me. Nevertheless, not my will, but yours, be done" (Luke 22:42 ESV). That is what it looks like to honor one's Father and mother, and the entire family of the human race. That is why he is not ashamed to call us brothers and sisters, even as we curse and yell at him for not pleasing us with our pettish wishes.

But I could not get the sixty-year-old dad out of my mind. As soon as I finished translating for the young man's attorney, I walked out of the courtroom and ran after the father. I caught up to him right outside the courthouse door. I had no idea what I would tell him. But I awkwardly asked him, "What are you going to do now?" His eyes were still red, and his face was still wet from his tears. But he did not hesitate. "I'm headed to jail, gonna put some thirty bucks in his account. I'm sure he can use it for some extra food. He likes to eat something before he goes to sleep. Maybe he'll also call me. He yells and cusses at me, but I still like to hear his voice." Now it was my turn to get teary eyed. The man reached for me, and we embraced. I sensed that he needed to hug somebody, and at that moment, so did I.

It almost seems superfluous "to draw the spiritual application."

But what if Jesus had been asked after leaving Pilate's court-yard, where he was lashed, spat, and beaten, "What are you going to do now?"

What would have been His answer?

"Well, I'm headed to justify those soldiers that just gave me this beating, spat on me, and pounded this crown of thorns on my head. Gonna give my life for them, gonna forgive them so as to make them right again before God. They're all covered with the scars of their own sins. Gotta cover them with my righteousness; it's too cold and dark for sinners all over this world. This cross is kinda heavy, but nothing like the sins they carry. On this cross, I'll take their sins on my body. That will justify them forever, and put them right with God. I don't like it when they cuss and spit on me, but there's no other way to present them whole before their Father. On that cross, it's all about them. I must become just like them before God. That way, I will bear their sin. Every blow and every bit of spit just lets me know how much love and forgiveness they need. I wish they would call me afterward. But they don't need to. I'll be calling on them, yes, you can be sure of that. I'll be calling on them, day and night. Gotta go now. There's a lot for me to do up there on that hill yet, and gotta finish it, clear to the very end. All sinners must know that they have been forgiven and justified . . ."

And so, on he walked up the hill to the Place of the Skull, his shoulders trembling from all the weight . . .

20

The Hug of God

"In this hope we were saved . . . So what are we going to say about these things? If God is for us, who is against us? He didn't spare his own Son but gave him up for us all. Won't he also freely give us all things with him?" (Romans 8:22-24, 31-32 CEB).

He was just eleven years old, but didn't hesitate to address the judge directly when he was brought to court. Very respectfully, trying to sound as grown up as he could, he addressed the court. "Your Honor, when will I be able to go back with my mom?" His mother was at the far end of the courtroom, behind a closed off section. She was only thirty years old, but her appearance was like that of a woman far beyond her years. The skin on her face was wrinkled and twisted, characteristic of persons with a long history of drug abuse. Today she had been brought from a rehab center. The judge wanted an update on her progress. The medical report was not promising. She still suffered recurrent episodes of paranoid schizophrenia. She was still seeing things and hearing voices that just weren't there. She spent a lot of time talking out loud to unseen people. Eight months before, the Department of Social Services Child Abuse Prevention had removed the minor from her care. In one of her drug-induced schizoid episodes, she had beaten the child and pounded his head against a wall.

Now, months later, the child's feelings still went out to his "mom," and despite the hurt and betrayal of trust, he still loved her. At the foster home, the first thing he wanted to know every morning was "is my mom all right?" He could not shake himself free of his tender feelings for her. His foster parents were kind, but he missed his mother's warmth. In the courtroom, the mother looked at him as if trying to figure out who he was. This judge, normally talkative and ebullient, could not find words to answer the child. "Jimmy,[1] we hope it's soon, son; you must be patient for now." But the drama intensified when the child, in all innocence, once again stood, mustered all the courage and respect he could, and addressed the judge, "Your Honor, can I just hug her?"

Immediately the attorneys, social worker, the psychiatrist, the child's therapist, all huddled at the judge's bench. I could barely hear their whispered muffled concerns as they covered their mouths so the court microphone would not pick up their voices. "It's too early." "She could get violent with him here." "It would be too damaging to the child if she didn't even recognize him." "You'd have to order her handcuffs removed, I would oppose it", said the attorney for the department. "It's too risky." "There's no judicial precedent for that, Your Honor." I saw the judge shaking his head to the negative. Then, he finally addressed the child, "Son, I'm sorry you'll have to wait for that too."

How do you ask a child to wait when what he needs and wants is a hug from his mom at that very moment? What do you do with an ungiven hug? What do you do when your arms hurt not because of hugging but for a lack of hugging? One more look at his mom, and the child broke down in tears. With a glance from the judge toward the social worker, she escorted him out of the courtroom. As the door closed you could still hear the child's voice crying down the hallway, "Mommy, Mommy, I want my mom!"

Scripture says, "For we now know that all the creatures groan together and travail in pain together until now. And not only they, but ourselves also who have the first fruits of the Spirit, even we ourselves groan within ourselves, waiting for the adoption, that is to say, the redemption of our body. For in hope we are saved... What shall we then say to these things? If God is for us, who shall be against us? He that did not spare his own Son, but delivered him up for us all, how shall he not also give us all things with him?" (Romans 8:22-24, 31-32 JUB).

---

[1] The child's name has been changed to protect his identity.

There's a sense in which we also cry out, "How long before we go home to Mom and Dad?" All creation yearns and moans with that cry. Even Jesus in Gethsemane, in his cry to the Father, "Let this cup pass from me," seemed to be also saying, "I wanna go back home, Dad! But yet, he had to wait. And yes, it did seem like an eternity. An eternity of sins fell upon his soul. All our fears and anxieties fell on him. All our hatred and cruelty. All our misled attempts at love and being loved. And so, he needed a hug from his Father in his most desperate moment. In fact, his actual cry of "Daddy, I need a hug from you" is registered in Matthew 27:46, NCV. "My God, my God, why have you abandoned me?"

And as soon as he cried out with that shout from the deepest place of his soul, the religious experts huddled around the cross. "See? He's not God's Son. Otherwise he'd be strong and tough it out." "Well, that's fine, let's wait and see if his daddy comes down and gives him that hug." "He's not ready for a hug yet. Let him suffer a little longer for all the lies he's told." "He's really lost it now. He's far worse than we thought. If he really wants a hug, he's got to repent from teaching people that he forgives sins!" "He's had his chances to change and hasn't done a thing yet!" "And what's more, who'd ever want to hug him in that condition, anyhow?" "Hey, if you are indeed God's Son, quit crying out for hugs! In fact, you'll start feeling better if you come down from the cross, that hug-hungry feeling will go away!"

But he had to wait—not because of their mockery, but because of them, in fact because of us, for we were there in their disguise. And so, He died in hope, in the hope of that hug from his Dad, and in the hope of hugging us. "He trod the winepress alone," "saw the affliction of his soul, and was satisfied." He replaced his hunger for his Father's affection with the satisfaction of seeing us justified with his righteousness, and by carrying on his soul the iniquities of us all. So then, on the cross, instead of getting that hug from his Dad, he opened his arms and hugged us all into his Father's presence. What we still hope for is that eternal family embrace surrounded by our Father's everlasting loving arms. But this kind of hope does not disappoint, for the hug of God has been poured out into our hearts!

21

The Black Sheep

"The Lord says, 'Now, let's settle the matter. You are stained red with sin, but I will wash you as clean as snow. Although your stains are deep red, you will be as white as wool'" (Isaiah 1:18 GNT).

After the judge sentenced him, the young man sat down and opened his heart to me. "I'm the youngest of seven children. All my other brothers and sisters were sent to school; today they're all professionals. I am the black sheep of the family. I didn't do anything with my life. I only know how to work on menial jobs. I learned bad habits, made terrible friends. Now I'm about to lose my family. That night, I went home drunk. My wife bawled me out, so I shoved her around in front of the kids. Now they're all afraid of me. I think they hate me. I'm gonna do everything the judge tells me: the AA classes, the domestic violence program, the work program cleaning up the roads. I don't want to lose my wife and kids. They're all I've got left, if I've got them at all."

Tears were running down his cheeks, as he recounted his misdeeds at home, and how he'd wasted his life "doing nothing." But among all his tear-sodden phrases, one stood out, "I'm the black sheep of the family." I stood beside him in silence, praying for the right words, which weren't coming. My time with him was limited. Soon I'd be called to translate on another matter. On impulse I said to him, "Look, God does not have a fold of white sheep, and another fold of black sheep. God has only one-fold of sheep, and they're all black.

Before him, even our white wool is only a costume because He knows our truth; we're all nothing but black sheep. But Christ, our shepherd, gave his life for all the sheep; the black sheep who've never done anything with their lives, and the white sheep who've done nothing else but put on a good show, dressed up in white camouflage."

Throughout human history, there has only been one pure and white sheep, Jesus Christ, the Son of God, Son of man. He is that one and only perfect sheep, without spot or defect. He loves us with a love that is not ashamed to call us his brothers and sisters. In fact, on the cross he became a black sheep for us before God. That's the only way he could present us before God clean, pure, all dressed in the white wool of his perfect righteousness. The wool has been woven into an elegant mantle, exquisite in beauty, which covers all our spots and stains. The Old Testament already announced the impeccable quality of the Lamb of God. "Your lamb shall be without blemish . . . You shall not offer anything that has a blemish . . . to be accepted it must be perfect; there shall be no blemish in it" (Exodus 12:5 ASV; Leviticus 22:20,21 RSV). That is the reason why the Father himself testified that the Son had met that requirement on our behalf, "This is my beloved Son, with whom I am well pleased; listen to him" (Matthew 17:5 WEB).

But just as I was to excuse myself, quite satisfied with my offhanded evangelism, the young man called me back, "Wait, wait. What you said is all nice and good. Truth is, you don't know how black I really am. You already know why I'm here."

"Yeah," I retorted rather hurriedly.

But he continued. "This is not all the bad stuff I've done. It's not just what I did that brought me here. It's what nobody knows I did that makes me a really black sheep. If they were to find out . . ." he said with a glance toward the judge's bench, "I'd never get out."

His eyes pleaded with me to stay and listen to his story. I sensed a big confession coming for which I wasn't ready, but at that moment, the court deputy unknowingly came to my rescue. "Gotta bring another batch of custodies. Gotta take this guy back; he's already been before the judge." All I could manage was to point upwards with my index finger, cross my arms in a hug and point toward him. As he walked out the door cuffed and shackled, he managed a thumbs up from behind his back.

Probably just like you, I wondered to myself what was that big confession. The worst in me wanted to find out. But I never found out what happened to that young man or the confession that he thought would put him behind bars for the rest of his life.

However, it occurred to me that it is the nature of black sheep to convince themselves and everyone else how bad they really are, as if somehow that would make amends for their sin. But that has never worked for anyone, and never will. In fact, there's no need to convince anyone, not even God, for He already knows. God knows not only all we've done, but all we're capable of doing. And yet, even for Him, there's only one confession he needs to hear. "If you confess with your mouth that Jesus is Lord and believe in your heart that God raised him from the dead, you will be saved. For with the heart one believes and is justified, and with the mouth one confesses and is saved" (Romans 10:9,10 ESV).

A prisoner's confession (aren't we all prisoners?) may even serve a cathartic purpose, which is perhaps what the man of our story was after, although at greater harm to himself. So, the cathartic value of confessions may rightly be questioned. But the purpose of "confessing with one's mouth that Jesus is Lord" goes beyond catharsis. When one confesses with the mouth that Jesus is Lord, one is in fact confessing, as Luther put it, "my whole life, and all that I do, act, speak, and think, is such as to be deadly and condemnable." Thus, my "blacksheepfulness," although it saturates my very nature, does not lord over me because I have confessed that Jesus is Lord. My sin is not the last word over me. The last word over my "blacksheepfulness" is the perfect Lamb of God that takes away every defect or stain from me. My confession, even as a breath of faith, brings Christ's word of absolution, "Take courage . . . your sins are forgiven" (Matthew 9:2 TLV).

"The Lord says, 'Now, let's settle the matter. You are stained red with sin, but I will wash you as clean as snow. Although your stains are deep red, you will be as white as wool'" (Isaiah 1:18 GNT). Thinking of his own soul as that of a black sheep, the psalmist confessed, "The Lord is my shepherd, I shall not want" (Psalm 23:1 KJV). Hundreds of years later, a certain prophet in the wilderness confessed the stains of his own soul as he looked upon the spotless soul of Jesus when he cried out, "Behold the Lamb of God that takes away the sin of the world" (John 1:29 RSV). And Isaiah, previewing the cross, wrote:

"like a lamb that is led to the slaughter" (Isaiah 53:7 RSV). Thus, on the cross, that perfect Lamb took away the sin of all the black sheep, and those that only appear to be white. That's the way he formed his eternal fold; that's how we've been set free to "follow the Lamb wherever he goes" (Revelation 14:4 ESV).

22

The Judge's Wrath

"But God, being rich in mercy, because of the great love with which he loved us, even when we were dead in our trespasses, made us alive together with Christ—by grace you have been saved—and raised us up with him and seated us with him in the heavenly places in Christ Jesus, so that in the coming ages he might show the immeasurable riches of his grace in kindness toward us in Christ Jesus" (Ephesians 2:4-7 ESV).

A few weeks before, the defendant had shown up in court to answer charges for third time drunk driving. The public defender had argued successfully in his favor. "He hasn't committed any other infraction, misdemeanor, or felony. He's the sole provider for his wife and five kids. He's a supervisor in a large plant."

On the other hand, the district attorney argued that the man presented a serious risk to the community. "Any time, that drunkard will get behind the wheel again and kill some innocent victim. Worse, he could run into a school bus full of children. Your Honor, he must be kept locked up until his next hearing!"

The judge asked both attorneys to approach for a side bar, a confidential conference at the foot of the judge's bench. After a few minutes, the conference was over, and the judge addressed the defendant. "Look sir, I'm not going to lock you up, despite the well-founded objections of the district attorney. I'm offering you the deal of your life. I'm keeping you out of jail so you can work and provide for your family. But I'm going to impose several conditions. One, you are not going to drive anymore, period. It doesn't matter if you're sober, if you've had just one sip of alcohol, or even sniffed a glass of wine, until this matter is heard at the preliminary hearing. Walk, take the bus, ride a cab, but you are not going to get behind the wheel of a car. Not even if it's parked! Two, you're going to attend a *daily* session of Alcoholics Anonymous. Next time I see you, I want to see thirty-five signatures as proof of attendance on the AA card. Understood? I don't want any excuses. Drag yourself to the meetings if you have to. They have meetings at all hours of the day and into the night. Otherwise, I'll lock you up on the spot and give you all the jail time the district attorney is requesting, which is up to six years jail. And last, so that you know this is a great deal for you, I'm not going to require you to wear an ankle bracelet alcohol monitor. It is expensive, so save your pennies for your kids. Now, do we have a deal or not?"

"Yes sir, Your Honor," was the swift response.

"And how many AA meetings are you going to attend?"

"One every day, sir," once again, the immediate answer.

"And how many signatures on your attendance card?"

"Thirty-five, Your Honor," spot on response.

"And which excuse am I going to accept?"

"None, sir," was the reply, this time not quite as quickly.

But the judge was not finished. "What's going to happen in case you don't keep your part of the deal?"

"You'll lock me up right then and there, Your Honor."

"Don't doubt it for a second; glad you were paying attention," retorted the judge who then continued, "Do you see that gentleman over there?"

The judge was pointing to the court reporter. "Yes, Your Honor," this time more hesitantly.

"Do you know what he's doing?"

"Ah, no sir."

"Well, he's taking down every word of this deal. He's put on the record this entire conversation, and most importantly, your answers. I'll see you in about five weeks."

And so, smile on his face, our third time drunk driver left the courtroom apparently sober enough to face the responsibility of keeping his part of the deal.

Now, five weeks later, he showed up in court for his preliminary hearing, but with only *three* signatures on his AA card. His public defender merely shook his head, and handed the card to the judge. As the judge took one glance at the card, a mischievous sneer formed on his face. "Ah, my friend," he quipped. And then to the Court Reporter: "Carl, do you have the transcript of my conversation with this gentleman about five weeks ago?"

"Yes, Your Honor."

"But, Your Honor," interrupted the defendant. "It's that my mother got gravely ill, and I had to leave the country to go see her."

No sooner had the reporter read the last word of the transcript, then the judge, still with that sneer on his face called to the bailiff, "Lock him up *now*!"

It's all in the transcript. Israel made a deal with God. They would obey the law, without a slipup, continually, and they would have life. The rest of the Old Testament is the transcript of the deal breakers, the litany of their excuses, and the resulting consequences. The Old Testament is a rehearsal of one enslavement into another; deals made, deals broken, constant relapses into slavery and oppression. That's the Old Covenant. But it's very much alive today. We've become experts at making deals with God. "Just teach me the right steps, and I'll make it happen." "Give me the power, and I'll be free." "With your help, I'll muster up what's deep within me to face whatever life throws at me. You'll see. You'll be proud of me."

Doesn't matter if we're believers on non-believers. Atheists and agnostics also make deals with the great, global human power they've substituted for God: "Trust us, we'll make it happen, we'll make things right, we'll fix the planet, we'll fix politics, we'll fix world hunger, unemployment, we'll fix illnesses, even old age, we can make eternal life happen ourselves. We just need a bit more time. That's our commitment; we are promise keepers. We'll extend human life to our solar system and beyond." But current social, political, economic, and military history is nothing but a transcript of broken deals across all human boundaries. Human history is nothing but a record of broken promises.

It's all bad news until we see Jesus climb up on that tree at Calvary. There he took humanity's enslavement, nailed to the cross, hanging by all four extremities. That was his way of embracing humanity across all latitudes and longitudes, tribes, tongues, and peoples, bearing humanity's loss of freedom, and eternal death. In so doing, he was humanity's only deal keeper, for that was his promise. "Christ brings a new agreement from God to his people. He brings this agreement so that those whom God chooses can have the blessings God promised, blessings that last forever. This can happen only because Christ died to free people from sins committed against the commands of the first agreement." (Hebrews 9:15 CSB). He was all—the deal maker, the deal broker, and the deal Keeper. But he does not bring that new agreement for us to sign again on the dotted line, pre-emptively signing our condemnation. He brings us the new agreement already kept and signed, on our behalf. He places it in our hands out of his over abundant grace, his sovereign will to save the lost. He stands before God as accused, guilty, condemned but at the same time, innocent, guiltless, and eternally alive.

Even the accuser says, "I find nothing in him" (cf. John 14:30). All promises kept, all commitments fulfilled, every work finished, perfect love is the signature in every cell.

And when the eternal judge calls for the transcript of his life, the global courtroom explodes in song: "Worthy is the Lamb, who was slain, to receive power and wealth and wisdom and strength and honor and glory and praise!" (Revelation 5:12 NIV).

23

You Haven't Done A Thing!

> "For you know the grace of our Lord Jesus Christ, that though he was rich, yet for your sake he became poor, so that you by his poverty might become rich" (2 Corinthians 8:9 NIV).

"You haven't done a thing. The judge ordered you to comply with forty hours of community service. How many have you done?"

"It's that I didn't have the money to sign up."

"He ordered you to sixty-five days of work release; that is, he sentenced you to sixty-five days in jail but gave you the chance to work them off without locking you up. How many have you done?"

"I didn't have the money to sign up for those either."

"Then he ordered you to the fifty-two week Domestic Violence program. How many meetings have you been to?"

"They want too much money upfront."

Struck and puzzled by his client's answers, the defense attorney nonetheless continued, "How do you know you can't pay for any of that? Did you show up at least to ask?"

"No. It's because money is very tight. I'm the sole provider for my two girls; I have sole custody. If I'm to do all that stuff, I'd have to leave my girls with a babysitter, and I haven't got the money to pay for one either."

"The judge told me he wants to lock you up right now for your failure to comply with his orders."

"But then my girls will have to stay home alone; Is that what the judge wants?"

"The problem is that you promised to comply with everything he ordered you, and you haven't done a thing!"

Finally, the judge gave him one week to find someone to care for his girls because he was going to get locked up for sixty days. "You'll have to turn yourself in next week. If you don't, I'll send the deputies after you, then you'll do at least a year. Don't worry about your girls. We'll lock you up, and your girls will be just fine in a foster home. Understood?"

We often hear about famous celebrities, business magnates, or sports personalities who create non-profit organizations. We're impressed by their large donations to fund various humanitarian foundations. Some organizations will research cures for cancer, other will fight social injustices, others will build housing for zones devastated by natural disasters, others will build and sustain children's hospitals—the list goes on. Sometimes we are awed at the personal worth of these individuals. But when compared to the actual amount donated for charity purposes, their personal worth astronomically exceeds the funds donated for humanitarian ends. Then, those in the know will publish the figures by which the donated amounts will actually reduce their tax obligations. When compared to the general population, they actually paid a tax amount far below the rest of the population. All thanks to all the good they did, are doing, and no doubt will continue to do! But one cannot avoid secretly concurring with the whispered comments that when compared to all the money they have, their deeds didn't amount to much! And even if they had given everything they had, as some have truly done, before God it counts for nothing.

But there was One who did give everything. Scripture says, "For you know the grace of our Lord Jesus Christ, that though he was rich, yet for your sake he became poor, so that you through his poverty might become rich" (2 Corinthians 8:9 NIV). What? Rich through his poverty? That's the mystery about the way debts are paid at the heavenly court. It's an inverted financial system. He became poor, the poorest of all poor, so as to gift us with a wealth that infinitely surpasses all material wealth.

"But where are those riches? Where do I find them? And, are they really given through grace, and by faith alone?"

"Ask, and it shall be given unto you." For the eternal judge is only requiring from you what you can only pay with the immeasurable sacrifice of his Son. He is eager to cancel all you owe. Just ask, believe, and receive; don't doubt it for a second. It is all yours. In the Son's shed blood, your account has already been overwhelmingly paid up. In his life, there's far more there than you could ever owe!

"But there must be some obligation on your part. Some condition."

Nada. Eternal accounts have a different accounting. You are a debtor of grace. Grace cannot be repaid. Grace can only be thanked. To the giver of grace is only owed gratitude, and even then, you could never be thankful enough. Even the response of thanks is not required. That also will be given unto you with a life lived in love and humility. Such a life will give you a new memory. It will always remind you that you love because he first loved you.

24

Sent To Jail By A Guitar

> "I have loved you with an everlasting love; therefore I have continued my faithfulness to you . . . He brought me to the banqueting house, and his banner over me was love" (Jeremiah 31:3 NRSV; Song of Songs 2:4 KJV).

They had been married for seventeen years. He was a professional guitar player. But on that Sunday afternoon, they were together and alone in the backyard. Beside him strewn on the ground, there were several empty bottles of beer. She was hanging the clothes up to dry; he was singing a heartbreak tune on his guitar. "Why are you singing that tune?" asked his wife.

"Because you're getting in bed with somebody else. I just know it. I've got a gut feeling about it. You've got a lover; I know it, who is it?"

"How does such a thing even occur to you? Don't say that, you know I've always been faithful to you . . ." was her response as she hung one of his shirts on the line.

"Ah, the only thing I don't know is his name. Tell me, who he is or I'll break your face!"

"Honey, what's going on? What's happening to you?"

"Don't deny it. I know it; you're cheating on me!" The argument increased in intensity, until he stood in front of her holding the guitar as if it were a baseball bat. "Tell me *now* who he is!"

"There's nobody, honey, please put . . ." But she didn't get to finish the sentence. He swung the guitar at her. Instinctively, she put her arm out to protect her face, but the edge of the guitar hit her arm and then rebounded on the back of her head. Immediately, blood gushed from her scalp and down her face. Her arm hung uselessly. The man ran out of the house while she stumbled next door. The neighbor called 911, and soon she was at the emergency room. They took nine stitches in her scalp, and the x-ray showed an oblique fracture of the left cubit.

Weeks later, the man, who was now detained, insisted to his attorney that it had all been nothing but an unavoidable accident. On the other side of the courtroom, the woman pleaded to the district attorney to level the heaviest charges against him and grant her a protective order restraining him from any contact with her for the rest of her life! The district attorney told her she would argue for attempted murder with life threatening injuries. That would carry a possible life sentence against her husband. So much for the romantic guitar player. Most likely his allegations weren't true, but nothing would ever justify any kind of violence against a spouse, or anyone, in fact, for any reason. There's no song that could ever justify that kind of use for a guitar. He was eventually sentenced to thirty years to life.

The Psalms are songs, many of them accompanied by string instruments. The one appearing most often is the lyre, the ancestor of the guitar. For instance, the introduction to Psalm 6 indicates that it is to be sung "with string instruments," led by a "*sheminith*," an eight-string lyre. The *sheminith* was a carefully crafted instrument, no more than six to nine inches tall. It could only be played in two postures. Either kneeling with the instrument on the ground while you sang and plucked its strings, or with the instrument close against your breast. The first posture gave the impression that the musician was worshipping or pleading. The second made it seem as if the singer was playing from the heart.

It is with such pleading that our heavenly husband sings to us a love song. "He brought me to the banqueting-house, and his banner over me was love" (Song of Songs 2:4, ASV). In spite of all treachery, cheating, perversity, disdain, and unbelief, he keeps on loving us. Scripture says, "I have loved you with an everlasting love. I have drawn you with mercy" (Jeremiah 31:3 EHV). That mercy was already shown through his sacrifice on our behalf, on his own body on the cross. He was wounded for our rebellions, he suffered in our place, thanks to his wounds we have received peace . . . God let the punishment we deserve fall instead on him (Isaiah 53).[1] In fact, in Psalm 6 and its "twin" Psalm 38, David prophecies of the Messiah's suffering for us, but the context of the eight-string harp turns it into a love song. In both Psalms we hear the Messiah becoming sin for us, and thus he pleads on our behalf before the Father. He does not want us to hear it as his suffering, but as his love for us:

> There is no soundness in my flesh
> Because of Your anger,
> Nor any health in my bones
> Because of my sin.
> For my iniquities have gone over my head;
> Like a heavy burden they are too heavy for me.
> My wounds are foul and festering
> Because of my foolishness (Psalm 38:3-5 NLV).

This is one of the clearest descriptions of the Messiah becoming sin for us and carrying all our sinfulness before the Father. But he wishes to win our hearts by letting us hear his pleas as a love song for us!

This lover with his songs is the true love of our heart's desiring. Instead of violence against us, he took our pain on his own body. Instead of songs reminding us of our contempt and treachery, he sings to us of his eternal tender love. With those love songs, he wins over our hearts, knowing we will still not be faithful to him—no, nowhere even close to the meaning of faithful. Even so, our hearts so often doubt his love, even his existence! And when we do affirm his existence, often we wish he didn't exist at all. But he does not turn his back on us. Instead, he forgives, hugs, guides, and protects us with His Spirit. His love heals instead of wounds. In fact, we are healed by his wounds! His Spirit, that other Comforter, watches over us with a constant passion. From our hearts, He draws shouts and tears of happiness and praise! Against such love, there is no law that could ever condemn us. Instead, there is only grace that places love

---

[1] Author's paraphrase of Isaiah 53.

songs on our own lips. "He put a new song in my mouth, a hymn of praise to our God" (Psalm 40:3 NIV).

But wait! What are you doing just now? Seems like I hear you singing a love song. And, are you playing the guitar or an eight-string lyre? Doesn't matter, you've got a great voice,

> Sing that song over again to me,
> wonderful words of life,
> offer pardon and peace to all,
> wonderful words of life;
> beautiful words, wonderful words,
> wonderful words of life.[2]

[2] P.P. Bliss, "Wonderful Words of Life," *Baptist Hymnal 1991*, pp. 261-2. Hymnary.org, https://hymnary.org/text/sing_them_over_again_to_me_wonderful#instances. Public Domain.

25

Just Wait And See
What's Gonna Happen Now

"For God so loved the world that he gave his only Son, so
that everyone who believes in him might not perish but
might have eternal life" (John 3:16 NABRE).

In the interview with the public defender, she told a horrendous story
of physical, verbal, and emotional abuse. "I was so thankful to him
'cause he took me from extreme poverty and brought me here. I was
barely out of my teens with fanciful ideas about making a home with
him, with children, friends, a family of my own. But it wasn't long
before the abuse started. He wouldn't talk; he'd just hit. He would call
me by every name he could think of except my own name. Even when
the children came, he wouldn't stop. He doesn't give me a dime for
my personal things. He lies to the government about what he makes;
he's got several maintenance businesses going, but never even lets me
buy the groceries. If I ask him for a few dollars to buy bread, milk, and
eggs, he slaps me around. He says when we go shopping, what we buy,
and pays for everything. But if afterwards we run out of something,
then he takes it out on me again.

I've been with him ten years already, and I've always lowered my
chin. I've never talked back to him; I've never called the police on him.
But last week I had enough. It's true he had the nine-month-old in
his arms, but when he began insulting me like a dog, with his mouth
full of profanities; I don't know what happened to me. I was going to

slap him with all that I had, but stopped short as I touched his face. That's when he said, "Just watch and see what's gonna happen now." He called the cops on me. They came and since he knows the language better, he told them what happened, according to his story. The cops didn't even ask for my side of the story, arrested me, and took me to jail. Now they've also taken my kids away, put a restraining order on me, and he's practically left me out in the street. I've got nowhere to go. I don't know what I'm gonna do."

As I translated, I understood her desperation and helplessness. She felt torn apart. Her dreams of a home and family were destroyed. Now her children were under someone else's care—who knows who. Neither did she know how they were faring. Her sighs also spoke of an abusive husband who at one time had been the love of her life. The woman's tears kept on flowing as her defense attorney drew out her traumatic story.

But in the heavenly court, all is radically different. Our marriage to Jesus never disappoints. Scriptures quote from that different story, "My beloved is mine, and I am his" (Song of Songs 2:16 KJV). There's an unshakeable certainty in those words. A quiet confidence. The husband has shown his trustworthiness. The bride rests completely and confidently on his unfailing love. All human beings, regardless of how bereft of human love they may be, may indeed rest confidently in God's passionate love for them, a love that will not let them go. There's tender care at every step, even when times seem rough. He showed his trustworthiness at the cross. At the very place where in human terms he would have been justified in terminating the relationship, that's where he was cementing it forever! All his love is to be trusted, and it is ours given entirely by grace, and received by us through faith alone. He does not put conditions on his love because his nature is precisely to love unconditionally. Thus, his love forgives unconditionally, gives unconditionally, and justifies unconditionally. He even sends his Spirit to grant faith in him unconditionally. We may slap, despise, turn away, demean, and even slander his love, but his love is unfailing and will continually turn our way to save and forgive.

26

Reunified

> "He came to his own home, and his own people received him not. But to all who received him, who believed in his name, he gave power to become children of God" (John 1:11,12 RSV).

After twenty years of working in the courts, I had thought that I was immune to human pain, that nothing could move me to tears. But I still feel my eyes welling up with moisture when the judge rules that children must be removed from their own home and taken to a foster home. There's that look on the face of the parents that envelops the entire courtroom: remorse, failed love, sorrow, heart wrenching sobs, cheeks bathed in tears, eyes red and covered with tears, as the truth is revealed in pitiful sighs: "I didn't think I had belted him so hard," "I really didn't mean it," "Please forgive me, forgive me, give me another chance." However, the child protection court establishes certain requirements for parents if they wish to reunify with their children. The law gives the parents up to six months to attend parenting classes, individual and group therapy, and given the case, a drug rehabilitation program. During that time, the parents may have limited and supervised visits with their children. However, if the parents don't meet all these requirements, the judge may deem the children candidates for adoption. But when the parents have met all the requirements of the plan, there's a reunification hearing. Instead of tears of grief, there are tears of joy. It's a party of embraces, kisses, congratulations, hugs and more hugs. In some cases, even the judge provides cake and ice cream!

Scripture tells the story of the prodigal son, well known even out-side religious circles. However, the story is also inversely re-told in the numberless parents who abandon their children with the prodigal's own self-justification, "I just want to have a good time." How could that be? If our children are our future, there's nothing as priceless as those words full of affection, "Daddy, Mommy." There's nothing as precious as their innocent laughter and play. There are so many parents that turn their back on their greatest treasures so they can go chasing garbage heaps. Like the prodigal son, they also end up eating from pigpens. But before we cast too many stones, that's what we all do and have done with God. We turn our backs on the treasures of faith to go chasing after bubbles. But the story of the prodigal son – our own story – does not end in tragedy. In Christ, God became flesh and came to call us and bring us out from our hiding places. "He came to his own, and those who were his own didn't receive him. But as many as received him, to them he gave the right to become God's children, to those who believe in his name" (John 1:11,12 NASB1995). We were so lost we even crossed through the threshold of death's lair and didn't even know it! But Christ went in after us and pulled us from death's grip. "Since the children have flesh and blood, he too shared in their humanity so that by his death he might break the power of him who holds the power of death—that is, the devil—and free those who all their lives were held in slavery by their fear of death" (Hebrews 2:14-16 NIV). When Christ knocked down the stone of his grave, all of us walked out right behind him, free from the clutches of death. No longer to serve the agents of death, but to serve the calling of the Spirit. And the celebration? Look, the Judge himself is bringing out the goods. But this is no longer about cake and ice cream. Our celebration is with his own bread and wine, his very own life!

27

The Day Truth Was Punished

> "Therefore he is also able to save to the uttermost those who draw near to God through him, seeing that he lives forever to make intercession for them" (Hebrews 7:25 WEB).

One day a mother came before the judge requesting a restraining order against her husband. When she was called to the witness stand, her testimony was difficult to understand. Her voice trembled with tears as she told a story of abuse at the hands of her husband and father of three children. Father used the belt freely, mixing in slaps, kicks, and punches, knocking holes in the doors and walls. The judge's interest perked up when the mother told of the time the father had belted their eleven-year-old son. As the mother told the story, when the boy took refuge behind her, the father belted the mother on her legs, breasts, face, and finally when the mother turned away, he got to the boy. The judge asked if she had any witnesses, to which the mother said the boy himself would testify. Shortly, the boy was escorted from the hallway into the witness stand. The judge himself took up the questioning. The boy repeated almost word for word what the mother had said. But the father, who was present, had a very astute attorney.

Hiding her cynicism, she questioned the boy, "Tony, isn't it true that you love your mother very, very much?"

"Oh yes," said the boy from behind his worried and fearful face.

"Isn't it true that you would do anything to protect your mother?"

"Yes, I would," was the tearful answer.

"Isn't it true that you would say anything to make your mother happy?"

Another soft "Yes."

"That's it, Your Honor," concluded the attorney. "I stand by my client's innocence. This child has lied in order to protect his mother. It's totally understandable that he would, but my client does not have to suffer the consequences just to make mom happy. Who knows what she would do to him if he didn't!" obviously turning the allegations against the mother.

The judge believed the attorney's insinuations. He ruled that the minor had given false witness in order to help the mother, and did not issue the restraining order. As they left the courtroom, the boy cried, "But I told the truth, and the judge still didn't believe me! Now my dad's gonna beat me even harder!" In his innocence, the boy told the truth but was punished for his innocence. Was the boy telling the truth? We'll never know. But if he indeed was innocent, he lost his innocence on that fateful day when he could not protect his mother even by telling the truth.

God is not caught blind-sided by anyone's cleverness. God only listens to the heartbeats of innocence. But all human innocence is like a resounding gong or a clanging cymbal. Scripture affirms that even that innocent-looking newborn is conceived in sin, by two parents riddled with a sinful human nature. The most pious sounding innocence is nothing but static before God. There is only one heart, which from its conception until its death only beat with pure innocence before God: His own Son's. He was hated, persecuted, accursed, rejected, tempted—all the while blessing with love and forgiveness those whose sin and guilt he bore. He did indeed protect us with his innocence. In giving his life for us, he was a perfect witness of God's truth. He'd been sent by the Father to cover us with his innocence. When he gave his life for us, he was on the witness stand telling the truth about God's love. The Father does not judge on the basis of our guilt, but on Christ's innocence *for us*.

Christ's heart is like the sound system through which God hears humanity. But in his heartbeats, God only hears innocence, and thus, he cannot hear anything else but innocence from humanity. But don't leave yourself out of it because all this may sound so huge and encompassing. When the Father hears the innocence from the heart of Christ, he hears not your heartbeat of sin, but the heartbeat of Christ's innocence. It is yours by faith alone. "Therefore he is able to save completely those who come to God through him, because he always lives to intercede for them" (Hebrews 7:25 NIV).

28

He Just Slipped Out of My Hands

> "Because all the fullness of God was pleased to live in him, and he reconciled all things to himself through him; whether things on earth or in the heavens. He brought peace through the blood of his cross. Once you were alienated from God and you were enemies with him in your minds, which was shown by your evil actions. But now he has reconciled you by his physical body through death, to present you before God as a people who are holy, faultless, and without blame" (Colossians 1:19-22 CEB).

The twenty-two-year-old, dressed in his orange jail-issued jump suit, awaited his sentencing. Three years back, he'd spent his last cent buying a twenty-dollar baggie of meth cocaine. Two days later, it was gone. Some months before he'd taken a gun from a relative's house. Now was the time to carry out his plan. He went to the corner liquor store. Brandishing the gun, he yelled at the cashier to empty out the register. At the cashier's feet was his three-year-old son playing cars. Pointing the gun to the child, the assailant told the cashier to hurry up. The man immediately emptied the register and gave him about $500.00 (five-hundred) dollars in cash. As he took the money, he told the cashier that if he called the cops, he'd be "crying at the funeral of that little piece of "s**t" right there." Three days later, the emboldened thief just walked in, took a shopping cart and began helping himself to several cases of beer, cigarettes, liquor, and other goodies, all the while giving the cashier menacing looks. But this time the cashier was prepared. He'd installed a silent alarm. Minutes later, the police came and caught the thief red-handed as he pushed the cart out of the store . . . Now, three years later, the judge was calling the case to sentence the young thief. His mother in the audience wiped her tears with an already wet handkerchief. As I translated for her, she moaned, "When did he just slip out of my hands?"

Today, many accuse God that if he exists at all, humanity has slipped out of his hands. Humanity has turned out a most insolent child, assaulting all and everything, even himself. But at the beginning, God left human beings in charge of everything. He told our first parents, "Have many children and grow in number. Fill the earth and be its master" (Genesis 1:28 ICB). He created them with the best capabilities to preserve our planet as a paradise for all its creatures. But soon, the human being chose to slip himself out of his Creator's hands. He wanted to do things himself, choosing violence over love, death over grace, greed over gratitude. The result? Hatred, hostilities, struggles, wars, contaminating not only his own soul, but also even the air he breathed. But God intervened a little over two thousand years ago. He appeared unexpectedly in human flesh, as an infant in Bethlehem's stable. "For God was pleased to have all his fullness dwell in him, and through him to reconcile to himself all things, whether things on earth or things in heaven, by making peace through his blood, shed on the cross. Once you were alienated from God and were enemies in your minds because of your evil behavior. But now he has reconciled you by Christ's physical body through death to present you holy in his sight, without blemish and free from accusation" (Colossians 1:19-22 EHV). Once you have been reconciled by grace through faith, you shall never perish, and no one shall snatch you out of his hand. That's our new reality! Not even we will be able to slip out of his hands! We are forever safe in the Father's bosom.

29

What's best for the children?

> "Christ Jesus, who, being in the form of God, did not consider equality with God something to be grasped. But He emptied Himself, taking upon Himself the form of a servant, and was made in the likeness of men . . . He humbled Himself and became obedient to death, even death on a cross... that at the name of Jesus every knee should bow . . . and every tongue should confess that Jesus Christ is Lord, to the glory of God the Father" (Philippians 2:5-11 MEV).

The father, an undocumented alien from a foreign country. The mother, a citizen of the United States. He crossed the border, and after many plights was able to find a job as a gardener in a luxurious home. Then the unexpected happened. One of the young women in the home fell in love with him. Love brought along passion, and soon she gave birth to twin baby girls. Cinnamon skin, blonde, bright blue eyes. But the mother, instead of turning to the girls, turned to drugs. One day, she fell into a sting operation by local drug enforcement and was sent to jail. The amounts she was dealing were substantial, so she was sent away for several years. When her husband came home, she was already in jail, the girls were in a foster home, and an immigration agent was waiting for him. Soon he was deported to a border town. By law, Juvenile Court has to find the closest relative to care for the minors. Treaties between the two countries required the court to find the father, and eventually the authorities found him.

He lived in a plain brick house, but it was clean, had running water, lights, two bedrooms, but without any other amenities. On the other side of the border, the girls had been placed in a foster home. The parents were wealthy physicians, but childless, due to infertility issues. They gave the girls everything imaginable: dolls, dresses, dollhouses, televisions, huge teddy bears, bicycles; each girl had her own room, and had full run of the house. There was a large yard with swings, monkey bars, slides, a playhouse, and a kids' size swimming pool. Each girl even had her own babysitter! When the judge studied the custody requests, there was only one norm he had to consider. What's best for the children? Where would they be better off? The law always assumes that it is best for the children to be with at least one of the parents who does not have any pending problems with the law, and is legally permitted to be a caretaker. In this case, the lawyers for Juvenile Court alleged that the girls would be better off with their father, notwithstanding his economic status. He sold ice cream from a little cart in his hometown, and did other odd jobs to provide for himself. Further, the dad would give the girls what money could not give them: a father's love and affection. The foster parents' attorney argued that the girls had not only everything in the present, but a guaranteed future and the best education possible with their foster parents. Now, you be the judge. What's your verdict? What decision would you make?

But in the heavenly court, the decision was already taken. Our divine God became flesh and came to this earth in a manger, emptied of every earthly good. Even the ice cream vendors of this earth were better off. That is how God won his paternity claim over us. He divested himself of all divine privileges, adopted the humble status of a slave and was born a human being. Then he humbled himself in obedience to God, and died the death of a criminal on a Roman cross. But at his name, the name of Jesus, every knee would bow and every tongue confess that Jesus Christ is Lord to the glory of God the Father (Philippians 2:5-11). That is how he came to be the Father of all humanity, rescued the wicked from their evil and the pious from their pride. Today, he takes our hand and leads us to his home. God knows you and senses your fears, trembling faith, and doubts because of your sins and shortcomings. But he won't let go. That's what's best for you and me. Our past, present, and future is secure in him. He will never leave you nor forsake you—not even for an instant of our doubting faith.

30

Undone By The Judge's Questions

> "Enter not into judgment with your servant, for in thy sight shall no man living be justified" (Psalm 143:2 KJV). "As a father has compassion on his children, so the Lord has compassion on those who fear him" (Psalm 103:13 NIV).

At first glance, Juvenile Court for lesser infractions would seem to be of little consequence, until the judge himself becomes the investigator. A sixteen-year-old girl had received a summons for ditching school. The judge questioned the girl. "Tell me, what happened? You give me a good reason, I'll give you a break and throw out the fine."

"Well, it's that I missed the school bus."

"Alright, so tell me why."

"It's that I woke up late."

"Don't you have an alarm clock?"

"No, I don't."

"Don't you have a cell phone?"

"Yes, but it's my mom's, and I don't know how to use it."

"Then, how do you wake up?"

"My mom wakes me up."

Back in the section for the parents, I was translating for the mother. "Madam," asked the judge. "Do you wake her up on time?"

"Yes, I do, Your Honor."

Then the judge addressed the girl once again. "If your mother wakes you up on time, why can't you get to the bus stop on time?"

"It's that once my mom wakes me up, I drift back for a little snooze."

"So then, your mother doesn't come back to wake you up again, right?"

"Nope, she has to go to work."

"And the morning you missed the school bus was one of those mornings?"

"Yes."

"So once you got to the bus stop and the bus wasn't there, what did you do?"

"I kept on walking to school."

"And how long does that walk take you?"

"About half hour."

"But the police noted here on the summons that he stopped you one hour later, and you were still at the bus stop."

"Well, it's that I was thinking about walking all the way to school."

"So you didn't tell me the truth when you said you had kept on walking on your way to school."

"Hmmm, it seems like I didn't."

"So what were you doing all that time at the bus stop?"

"I was with some friends hanging out in the park . . ."

"Guilty! Twenty days of community service!" the judged exclaimed as he hammered the table with his gavel.

Scripture mentions that God considered David "a man after my own heart" (1 Samuel 13:14 NIV). But when this upright man thought that he'd have to face his Creator Judge, he pleaded, "Enter not into judgment with your servant, for in thy sight shall no man living be justified" (Psalm 143:2 KJV). How would you feel if this Judge would ask you probing questions about your faithfulness to your husband, your wife? What if he'd ask you what you really think about your teachers, co-workers, and your boss? What if he'd ask you about your honesty at work, in your homework, in your exams? What if he'd ask the children to tell the truth about all their excuses? Neither could we stand. Sooner or later, we would drop our chin.

Jesus, your Christ, is the only one innocent before God. But he is not going to roll you around with probing questions. He already knows all the answers. He just ignores your excuses and alibis. Instead, he comes before the Father and takes the heat for all your lies, big or little. He presents his life of truth, not yours. That is the evidence the Judge holds in his hands. On that basis, God forgives us. "As a father has compassion on his children, so the Lord has compassion on those who fear him" (Psalm 103:13 NIV).

31

What If You Were The Judge?

> "Enter not into judgment with your servant, for in thy sight shall no man living be justified" (Psalm 143:2 MEV). "As a father has compassion on his children, so the Lord has compassion on those who fear him" (Psalm 103:13 NIV).

Two families, close relatives. Three children. One judge decides. Two years before, the biological parents had lost custody of their children. They'd been arrested for use and sale of prohibited substances—illicit drugs. Juvenile Court gave the paternal grandparents custody over the children. At that time, the children were one, two, and three years old. Now the mother appeared before the judge requesting full custody of her children. Her arguments? She had over a year sobriety in a drug rehab program, had her own job, her own apartment; she claimed she'd turned around her life.

The maternal grandparents, who were called to testify, claimed that indeed it was true. When the children came over to visit the mother, they enjoyed their time with her. But when it was time to go back to the paternal grandparents' house they would cry and whine, even hide to avoid going back with them. On their part, the paternal grandparents claimed that the children now called them mom and dad, that the mother had not changed at all—perhaps at a later date— and that the children lacked nothing under their custody.

On the other hand, the mother refuted those arguments, saying the children's father was still using drugs and would show up high for his visits with the children. The man's parents claimed that before letting him in the house they would search him to see if he had drugs hidden in his clothes, and that he presented no danger to the children. The mother requested the judge to order drug testing for the dad before each visit with the children, and insisted she wanted full custody of her children.

Now, if you were the judge, what decision would you make? Do you grant the mother's petition, or do they stay with the paternal grandparents?

But at the heavenly court, the Judge takes a very radical decision. Our heavenly Father will under no circumstance consider sharing custody with the enemy of our souls, our bodies, and our very own existence. Our loving Father decides that he himself will adopt us as his very own children, all maternal and paternal families. All will be members of the one and the same family forever. Radical? Improbable? No way. In fact, that's what happened at the cross. There, Jesus paid the price for our adoption. Scripture says that, "he predestined us for adoption to sonship through Jesus Christ, in accordance with his pleasure and will" (Ephesians 1:5 NIV). Jesus Christ is our older brother, and he claims us as his own brothers and sisters within his own family. He did not adopt us because we were beautiful or intelligent, but because we "were dead in our trespasses and sins" (c.f. Ephesians 2:1). God's grace reminds us that we were adopted in someone else, in the body of Christ. Christ is the legitimate child. We have been adopted in him and for him. Apart from him we are children of wrath. "For he chose us in him before the creation of the world to be holy and blameless in his sight. In love he predestined us for adoption to sonship through Jesus Christ, in accordance with his pleasure and will—to the praise of his glorious grace, which he has freely given us in the One he loves" (Ephesians 1: 4-6 NIV). Yes! To the praise of his grace, because it's an irrevocable adoption. We belong to the family of the universe forever to the glory of his praise!

32

Innocent Until Proven Otherwise

> "For just as through one man's disobedience many people were made sinners, so also through one man's obedience many will be made righteous." (Romans 5:18-19 ISV)

The judge was instructing the jury before a trial. "There's the accused. He has been charged with the rape of a minor. It is a felony with several enhancements. The law requires you to be the triers of the evidence. You must hold the defendant innocent until proven otherwise beyond a reasonable doubt." At that point, a murmur was heard from the audience in the courtroom, from the section where the victim's family was seated. They already held him guilty. Now, as the trial begins, the judge is asking the jury to hold that pervert as guiltless? The judge continued unperturbed. "You must not take into account the fact that he has been arrested and charged with this crime. When determining his guilt or innocence, you must weigh only the testimony given by the witnesses in this matter. Jury number Five, at this moment, are you able to hold the accused as innocent?"

"Well," responded Five, "my opinion is that where there's smoke, there's fire. If he's sitting there, it must be for a good reason."

The judge continued, "Jury number Ten, right now if you were asked to give your opinion about the accused, what would you say, guilty or not guilty?"

Ten responds, "Frankly, he looks guilty, and that he was arrested for a heinous crime like this, I would say more likely, he's guilty."

The judge then responded with a question, "So the two of you, without hearing any witness or weighing any evidence, are ready to hand down a guilty verdict? What about if the matter turns out to be a case of mistaken identity?"

But before the heavenly throne, there's no such thing as the presumption of innocence, but the presumption of guilt! We are all held as guilty until a life is brought forward as evidence of a life displaying purity, righteousness, overflowing with selfless love, without defect, full of constant faith, free from all doubt, without wavering in its convictions even for the most fleeting moments. There's no place at that moment for the presumption of innocence since "all have sinned and come short of the glory of God" (Romans 3:23 KJV). There's no need for the slightest bit of evidence to be brought against us. Adam's guilt is enough. Due to Adam's sin, God declared that we are all guilty and merit eternal death. With our own thinking and living, we only give evidence that we have the same parent, Adam. "Consequently, just as one trespass resulted in condemnation for all people, so also one righteous act resulted in justification and life for all people. For just as through the disobedience of the one man many were constituted sinners, so also through the obedience of one man many will be constituted righteous" (Romans 5:19-19 NIV). Before God, no one can say, "it's a case of mistaken identity." We are all "just like our dad." Rebellious, hypocrites, fakers, thieves, even assassins, if not in deed, then in thought. That is why we need the life of another to take our place before God, and that life is in his Son. In him there is infinite righteousness, a boundless love without conditions, a grace that reaches and overtakes even the most perverse and twisted heart. That righteousness that is in him is ours for the taking by faith alone. There's no expiration date to the offer. He is the only one with the presumption of innocence and that life is the gift offered to you by God. Open your hands to receive it and offer God nothing in return, for then there won't be room for all the righteousness you need. Confess it today, "Jesus took my guilt, I am innocent before God in him."

33

Children in The Hands of Fools

"I will not leave you orphaned, I will be with you to the end of the world. I will not leave you nor forsake you. Don't fear or be dismayed, I am the Lord your God, and will be with you wherever you go. My peace I give to you, my peace I leave with you. Let not your heart be troubled, neither let it be afraid" (John 14:18 NRSVA; Matthew 28:20 CEV; Joshua 1:5 NKJV; John 14:27 ESV).

Almost always, in Juvenile Hall, when the judge orders the children to be removed from their mother, the mother reacts with great desperation. There are tears, cries, sighs, asking anxiously when and how she can visit her children. But this occasion was an exception. The mother, with a very pleased look on her face, leaned her head on the shoulder of the young man at her side. He was very good-looking, corpulent, strong with light brown eyes and short wavy hair. His hand gently caressed the mother's hands while they answered the attorney's questions. The children had already been detained, but there was no look of anguish or desperation on the mother's face. The incident unraveled slowly through the attorney's questions. There were two boys, one seven, the other five. According to the couple, that night the lights went out in the area due to a lightning storm. It was late so the couple decided to go out and buy flashlights, leaving the children home alone. But, whose home? At the house of the wife of that charming, good-looking young man! He was not the father of either one of the children, or the husband of the affectionate young woman.

They were lovers. On the other hand, the young man's wife worked the night shift at a nearby casino and would not return until morning. But she fell ill and decided to come home. When she opened the door, she found two strange children fast asleep on her sofa. Soon after, the young man showed up with his girlfriend, the children's mother. You can imagine the scandalous scene! Shouts, screams, yelling, things thrown around. A neighbor heard the raucous disturbance and called the police. The agents accused the mother of negligence; the children were detained. That was the end of that marriage for the young man, and goodbye to his girlfriend's children. Fury and betrayal for the cheated wife. But a very pleased mother next to her boyfriend in the lawyer's hearing room.

The divine Judge made a covenant with the Son. He would come to this earth to seize guardianship away from the one who had kidnapped and enslaved us. This guardian usurper had abandoned us to the darkness of our own hate, selfishness, and constant frenzy. The Son became flesh, and beginning at the manger, he sought us until he found us at the cross. A scandal ensued, for many are offended even at the idea of "God's Son," and much more with a cross, spilled blood, a sacrificed life given as ransom for sin. But no matter whom it offends, that is how we were rescued and transported to the Kingdom of the Son. There, by his grace, we have already entered into our new home. In this home, there is no doubt as to the identity of our Father. There is no DNA test needed to establish proof of paternity. It is enough to look at the scars in his hands, his side, his feet. One only needs to receive the evidence of his fatherly and motherly care with which God deals with us. "I will not leave you orphaned, I will be with you to the end of the world. I will not leave you nor forsake you. Don't fear or be dismayed, I am the Lord your God, and will be with you wherever you go. My peace I give to you, my peace I leave with you. Let not your heart be troubled, neither let it be afraid" (John 14:18 NRSVA; Matthew 28:20 CEV; Joshua 1:5 NKJV; John 14:27 ESV).

34

Beer in The Baby's Bottle?

"So Jesus said to them, "Truly, truly, I say to you, unless you eat the flesh of the Son of Man and drink his blood, you have no life in you. Whoever feeds on my flesh and drinks my blood has eternal life, and I will raise him up on the last day. For my flesh is true food, and my blood is true drink. Whoever feeds on my flesh and drinks my blood abides in me, and I in him" (John 6:53-56 ESV).

The mother's hand gestures mimicked the emptying of a can of beer into a baby bottle. "That's why I had to snatch the baby bottle from him. Otherwise, he would have let the baby suck on beer. That's happened more than once, I'm sure. I don't know if he's done it behind my back, but I was always watching from the corner of my eye. James is almost always drunk; that's why he also wants to get the baby drunk. But the baby is only a year and a half. That's why I'm requesting this Stay-away order. It all began when we were celebrating the boy's first birthday. James got drunk first, just before the party started. When the guests arrived with their children, he was already staggering and mumbling as he greeted them. I didn't know what to do. At the end when we gathered for the cake, he took the can of beer from his hand, poured it into the baby's bottle, and put it in his mouth. Whether the baby sucked the beer or not, I don't know, but everyone started screaming. I ran over, pulled the bottle from the baby's mouth, grabbed the can from his hand, and wiped the baby's mouth. I began to cry with the baby at my side, but James grabbed him and drove away drunk like he was. Then he came back later, and proceeded to kick me and the baby out of the house. He left us out in the street. We walked a mile under the hot sun to a friend's house. That's why I'm now requesting a Stay-away order, and for him to leave the house." That was no happy birthday on that failed party. What's there to celebrate in hate, selfishness and beer in a baby's bottle?

But how would Joseph and Mary celebrate Jesus's first birthday? The Jews of that time didn't celebrate the first *birthday*, but the first *Passover*. They probably had unleavened bread with bitter herbs. Some twenty-nine years later Jesus celebrated his own Passover, the new covenant he made on our behalf. It is a unique covenant, which no one else can make, sealed by his own blood on the cross. Then he made us guests at his table celebrating the fulfillment of that covenant, all through sheer grace. It's as if he took the cup and placed it at our lips. Nothing toxic there, but life giving. "Then He took the cup, and after He gave thanks, He gave it to them, saying, "Drink of it, all of you. For this is My blood of the new covenant, which is shed for many for the remission of sins. I say to you, I will not drink of this fruit of the vine from now on until that day when I drink it new with you in My Father's kingdom" (Matthew 26:27-29 MEV). You and I will be there. The mother and the baby of our story will be there. The baby's father will be watching from the back, so as not to embarrass us for our hypocrisy. But our heavenly Father will be celebrating with great joy, overwhelmed with love for his redeemed children. He gives us the cup we don't deserve, the cup full of grace and forgiveness. But the Son took the cup that we *do* deserve: the bitter cup of our sins mixed in with God's purifying wrath. That took place in his body, not in ours. That is why he said, "Jesus said to them, "Truly, truly I say to you, unless you eat the flesh of the Son of Man and drink His blood, you have no life in you. Whoever eats My flesh and drinks My blood has eternal life. And I will raise him up on the last day. For My flesh is food indeed, and My blood is drink indeed. Whoever feeds on my flesh and drinks my blood abides in me, and I in him" (John 6:53-56 ESV). That's how he celebrated our birthday into eternal life!

35

She's Not My Daughter

> The Spirit you received does not make you slaves, so
> that you live in fear again; rather, the Spirit you received
> brought about your adoption to sonship. And by him we
> cry, "Abba, Father" (Romans 8:15 NIV).

"And now that you've hitched up with that other one, and the girl
bothers her, don't you want her for your daughter anymore? Now
she's a bother? After all your battles in court to get her custody that
you even lied to the judge, she's now a nuisance?"

All this was taking place before the judge, who was having a
hard time controlling the now separated couple. They had never
married. But now she was filing for child support and that he should
have no court ordered visitation with his daughter. Previously, the
young man had treated the five-year-old girl like his daughter. But
now before the judge, he claimed the girl was not his, and that
when he'd started living together with the young woman, she was
already pregnant with the girl from "heavens knows who." But
when the baby was born, he'd signed the birth certificate claiming
her as his own, for the mom's sake only, for he'd known all along
the baby wasn't his. Now he claimed he was not the girl's father,
and, thus, had no obligation to pay for child support and had no
reason to have mandated visitation with a girl who was not his
daughter.

The judge asked him, "Does the girl call you 'Dad'?"

"Well, that's what her mother tells her to call me."

The judge, unperturbed, continued. "Did you ever call her 'daughter'"?

"Well, only when she was little, but not anymore 'cause I don't want her to think I'm her dad. So, Martiza is not my daughter."

The judge's face took on a different look. "Look, young man. Children are not toys that you can just throw into the garbage when they're no longer of any use to you. Before the law, before the girl, and you yourself, you are the father. Pay the indicated child support and visit with your daughter. You are the only dad she has!"

Our Lord Jesus Christ fell in love with us when we were still "dead in our sins and trespasses" (Ephesians 2:1). Even though the arch deceiver and enemy of God, the devil and accuser claims us as his children, Jesus did not leave us in his despotic hands. He went to the cross and forever snatched us away from our fake father. He himself adopted us as sons and daughters and gave us his entire inheritance. "The Spirit you received does not make you slaves, so that you live in fear again; rather, the Spirit you received brought about your adoption to sonship. And by him we cry, 'Abba, Father.' The Spirit himself testifies with our spirit that we are God's children. Now if we are children, then we are heirs—heirs of God and co-heirs with Christ, if indeed we share in his sufferings in order that we may also share in his glory" (Romans 8:15-17 NIV).

This becomes real to us when notwithstanding all our doubts and conflicts, we believe we are his daughter, his son—that we are not abandoned to the whims of luck in this world without anyone to love and understand us. Neither God's mood nor his will to love us changes from day to day. But this is what the deceiver would like for us to believe. That today God loves us, but tomorrow he may not; and thereafter we could be abandoned forever. If we believe Satan's lies, we fall into the claws of a destroyer and not a Savior. But we do have a dad, and forever! The evidence? The blood of his Son, Jesus, given at the cross was the price of our redemption, the price of our adoption. His oath to take us as his children is irrevocable; it cannot be taken back. We are his children forever!

36

The Out-Of-Control Pastor

"For it is by grace you have been saved, through faith—and this is not from yourselves, it is the gift of God—not by works, so that no one can boast" (Ephesians 2:8-9 NIV).

He was a young pastor, fresh out of seminary, getting started in a large church as youth and children's pastor. Everything was going well until Francesca started coming to the youth group. The thirteen-year-old girl was incorrigible, uncontrollable; she cussed, talked back, disrespected, full of mischief and energy. The mother had sent her to church as a last resort. At her first entrance, everything changed in the youth group. Nacho, the pastor, soon began to lose his patience. Francesca took over the group and had them laughing, making faces, sounds and moans, mocking the young pastor, the Bible, and every authority invoked. Until one day, Nacho totally lost it. In front of the entire group, she cussed him, and he responded with a couple of slaps, thinking that would calm her down. Pulling her by the hair, he finally sat her down. Finally, Chesca calmed down . . . but not for long. When she got home, she told her parents what had happened. Before sundown, the police showed up at the young pastor's home. Yes, they arrested him, took him to the police station and booked him for assaulting a minor. He was freed on his own recognizance and promised to show up in court to plead before the charges. The judge sentenced him to an anger control management program, fined him $2,000 for damages to the girl, and forty hours picking up trash on the freeways. If he met all these conditions within ninety days, his record would be expunged, cleaned, as if nothing had happened. Fair punishment or too much leniency? You be the judge. But the young pastor met every requirement of his sentence, and his record was wiped cleaned. What's more, the church granted him grace and reinstated him as youth pastor.

Oh, that it would be that easy to wipe our record before the heavenly court! That with a few good works, we could get the Judge of the Universe to wink away our sin. But our heart is so desperately wicked that we would quite piously present our complaints and excuses as our defense before God.

"What? Didn't that girl get what she deserved? Wasn't it about time that someone gave her some discipline? I should have been given a medal instead of community service. Now she's going to finally respect God's house. What, me? A minister of God, with a seminary degree picking up broken beer bottles along this dangerous freeway? My time is much more valuable; I should be teaching God's word to those truly sinful. God, why did you send that girl to my youth group anyhow? You knew what was going to happen."

And so on. Do we even think we can justify ourselves with that internal dialogue? We cannot erase our heavenly record with good works because our inner talk condemns us. God only accepts a perfect record, clean from any previous crimes, and all sins of thought and intentions. There is no human being that can make an appearance before the judgment seat of God. But one does appear: Jesus Christ, Son of God, son of man, who was sent to take our place. He presents his perfect life as a substitute for our own. It is not his heavy hand that "calms us down." He wins us with his intense, persistent love. "For it is by grace you have been saved, through faith—and this is not from yourselves, it is the gift of God—not by works, so that no one can boast" (Ephesians 2:8-9 NIV). That is how the Lord quietly shuts our blaspheming mouths, how he calms us down by looking at the cross, and from there tells us, "You were lost like a wandering sheep, but I was here for you all this time, taking your place."

37

From Just Teasing To Falling In Love

> "I have loved you with an everlasting love; I have drawn you with unfailing kindness . . . I drew a picture of you on my hand. You are always before my eyes" (Jeremiah 31:3 NIV; Isaiah 49:16 ERV).

The thirty-five-year-old man insisted before the judge to grant him a restraining order against a woman of about the same age. When the judge asked him to offer his reasons, he answered, "It's that she won't leave me alone. She follows me everywhere; she's always calling and texting me."

"But that's no reason at all to grant a restraining order. Your life is not in danger. You don't need that kind of protection," answered the judge. "She's not assaulting nor threatening you. Do you have any other reason?"

"Yes," said the man, "this letter."

The judge asked me to translate the letter: "My dearest love, I confess that what began with just teasing at work soon became the strongest love for you. I don't want you to abandon me. Don't forget me ever. I will always love you. Please forgive me, for I sound like a little girl confessing my love to you . . ."

"Stop, stop," said the judge. "Don't read any more. There are no threats there, not even insults. It's just a love letter."

"Yes, Your Honor, but it's that I no longer want anything to do with her."

"Well," said the judge, "it's that I cannot dictate over your feelings or hers. There's just no legal foundation for the restraining order."

He then addressed the woman who had been ordered to be present: "Do you still want anything to do with him?"

"No," she answered coldly.

"And you, sir, do you want anything to do with her?"

"Of course not, sir."

"Then the matter is closed. Next case, please."

But once out of the courtroom, the man took me aside and told me the underlying drama. "It's that I'm married; I've got two precious girls. I made a huge mistake in getting involved with that woman. Now I can't get her off my back. But even during our affair, she got involved with somebody else. My wife has always been faithful to me, but now she's asking for a divorce, and the girls don't even want to see me. I lost my home for getting fooled over a false attraction. My wife told me, 'Get a restraining order against that woman, or it's over.' But now the judge didn't grant it. I don't know what I'm going to do, or what she's going to say now. I hope I can convince her to stay."

That's the way we are before God and neighbor. Unfaithful, fickle, we let ourselves get carried away by false attractions. Too late we realize we've lost everything. But God finds us in our misery. The way he heals us is bold, risky. He offers us a love that is much more passionate that any other passion or love we could ever find. It's the love of his Son, who replaces our misery with the infinite riches of his grace and forgiveness. He is no betraying lover offering us some cheap love and pleasure. He persists until he finds us, and against that love, there is no restraining order. Nothing can keep him away. "I have loved you with an everlasting love; I have drawn you with unfailing kindness . . . I drew a picture of you on my hand. You are always before my eyes" (Isaiah 49:6 ERV). "All the love of my Son is yours, his life, his death, his faithfulness, his purity, it is all yours. I know I will win your heart over!" "Many waters cannot quench love, neither can floods drown it" (Song of Songs 8:7 NRSV). "What will separate us from the love of Christ? Will trouble or distress or persecution or famine or nakedness or danger or sword? ... For I am convinced that neither death nor life, neither angels nor rulers, neither things present nor things to come, nor powerful forces, neither height nor depth, nor anything else in creation, will be able to separate us from the love of God in Christ Jesus our Lord" (Romans 8:35,38-39 EHV).

38

Fourth Stage Terminal Cancer

> Bless the Lord, oh my soul, and forget not all his bene-
> fits. He is the one who pardons your iniquities. He is the
> one who heals your wounds. He rescues your life from
> the tomb and covers you with love and compassion . . .
> He does not deal with us according to our sins . . . He
> remembers that we are but dust (Psalms 103:2,3,10,14).[1]

It's not a phrase you expect to hear in traffic court. There, everything has to do with demands and obligations, and how they've been broken. Fines are handed down, orders to appear at trial, traffic school, guilty and not guilty pleas. But, who pleads, "I've got cancer"? Even so, there was a man about sixty years old, tall, handsome, still showing good health, but a profound sadness marked his eyes and every line of his face. He was accused of several traffic infractions: ran a stop sign, using a cell phone while driving, seat belt violation. When the judge asked him how he pled, he responded firmly but gently, "Your Honor, I've just been diagnosed with fourth stage lung cancer. It's now all over my body. I plead with you to forgive my fines." A profound silence enveloped the courtroom. Even the judge kept silence before a sentence that only life hands down: the sentence of dwindling hopes.

Finally, the judge broke the silence. "Do you have medical evidence for your situation?" The defendant took some papers from a folder and handed them to the judge. After a brief reading, the judge

---

[1] Author's paraphrase: Psalm 103: 2,3,10,14.

answered, "Well sir, your fines are exonerated. You don't owe anything. As long as you are able, please drive carefully."

At the divine throne of justice, our situation is not much different. We have the cancer of sin all over our being. The symptoms?
Rebelliousness toward God . . . confidence that, if there is a God, he
will realize we're not that bad and won't refuse our entrance to eternal life. We're also quick to judge others, and even secretly envying
others' apparent success in evil and sin. Such evil is so attached to
our being that as the man in our story, we cannot pay the debt before
God, because our illness has no cure. But humanity's history does
not end with those foreboding overtones. The story of the passion of
Christ is more than just a story. It's the living reality of the one who
took on our cancer and carried it on the purity of his own soul. It's
the reality of him who suffered our pain and took on our brokenness.
Scripture comforts us with the words, "And with his stripes we are
healed" (Isaiah 53:5 ASV). So on the cross, he not only paid our fine,
he took our cancerous soul on his own being in order to cover the
totality of our being with his own health and well-being, which is his
love, righteousness, and holiness. So that everyone who confesses the
name of Jesus can claim before the divine judgment seat: "I had the
cancer of sin all over my body, but he took it away, and granted me the
perfect health of his entire life. I am now here without spot or wrinkle." Hard to believe? Such is God's grace. It is so immense it cures
even us. Bless the Lord, oh my soul, and forget not all his benefits.
He is the one who pardons your iniquities. He is the one who heals
your wounds; he rescues your life from the tomb and covers you with
love and compassion . . . He does not deal with us according to our
sins . . . He remembers that we are but dust (Psalms 103:2,3,10,14).[2]

---

[2] Author's paraphrase: Psalm 103: 2,3,10,14.

39

Your Son Died, You Owe Nothing

> "For Christ's love compels us, because we are convinced that one died for all, and therefore all died. And he died for all, that those who live should no longer live for themselves but for him who died for them and was raised again" (2 Corinthians 5:14-15 NIV).

Two years after her son's death, she was still wearing black. In the courtroom, her elegant black dress with black lace accents generated a sense of awe and quiet respect. There was no small talk and the nervous, muffled laughter usually heard at the beginning of traffic court. When the judge took the stand, the first name he called was Matthew Broward.[1] But the lady in black stood up and approached the stand. "Your Honor," she affirmed with trembling voice, "My son cannot be here because he passed away two years ago. I have his death certificate here."

The bailiff quickly took the document and delivered it to the judge. "And, how can I help you, madam?" replied the judge.

"I'm here to pay my son's debts. He had four traffic summonses. According to these tickets, he owes $2,500.00 dollars in traffic fines."

"Lady," the judge answered slowly, "your son died; you owe nothing."

"But Your Honor, it's my responsibility to pay all of my son's outstanding debts. How would you like me to pay for these fines? I've brought all the money with me."

---

[1] A fictitious name.

The judge answered again, this time more emphatically. "Lady, you owe nothing. Pay nothing. Your son has died. A dead person owes nothing because he's unable to pay. He's dead."

"But Your Honor, it's that as a mother, I don't feel right that my son left these debts open. I need to pay them."

"Lady, lady. Hear me out. The law requires that when someone dies, all traffic debts be exonerated." The judge motioned to the bailiff who had to escort her to the door, for she kept insisting that she had to pay for her son's debts.

When Jesus died on the cross, we all died in him. Whoever believes this, owes God nothing. Why? Because a dead person owes nothing and is unable to pay anything. Scripture says we were all "dead in our sins and trespasses" when he paid our debt; it was only then that he made us alive in Jesus Christ. That's the law of the gospel. When he died, we all died. It's the simplest confession of faith, but the heart barely dares to believe it. We all walk around in black, wanting to pay debts we don't owe. "For God so loved the world, that he gave his only Son, that whoever believes in him should not perish, but have eternal life" (John 3:16 ESV). "For Christ's love compels us, because we are convinced that one died for all, and therefore all died. And he died for all, that those who live should no longer live for themselves but for him who died for them and was raised again" (2 Corinthians 5:14-15 NIV). We live again, not so that we will now pay our debt, but to proclaim that we live because our debt was paid! We're no longer alive, trying to pay off our debts. That will only start the billing all over again! As in our story above, the Son died; thus there are no debts pending against us. What then, do we do? Sing, whistle, dance, paint, practice a sport, do good to your neighbor, worship, live a life of worship to him. Your debt has been forgiven. The Son has died on the cross, and we died with him. And when he rose from the dead, we rose as well in him. All bills have been cancelled, no matter how high the bill. Even more, we now bask in the wealth of the great treasure of his riches. But if you disbelieve it, then believe it while still in your unbelief! However, you can always try to pay what you don't owe. No matter how much you pay, it will amount to nothing. Everything you attempt to put in heaven's bank account will bounce. The currency is bad. Heaven only knows the currency of Christ's life, death, and resurrection! Praise God. Your sins, which are many, have been forgiven.

40

What Is Your True
And Correct Name?

> "As I live, says the Lord God, I have no pleasure in the death of the wicked, but rather that the wicked turn from his way and live . . . I have come that they might have life, and have it more abundantly . . . If death ruled because of one person's failure, those who receive the multiplied grace and the gift of righteousness will even more certainly rule in life through the one person Jesus Christ" (Ezekiel 33:11 MEV; John 10:10 NMB; Romans 5:17 CEB).

The woman at the stand was testifying in an attempted murder and armed robbery case. She had been the cashier at a convenience store. One day a man ran in and brandished a gun in her face: "Give me all the money, now!" The thief, almost brushing her face with the weapon, yelled at her, "Move it!" But the cashier did not cower. Drawing courage from her fear, she let out such an ear-piercing scream that the thief turned around and ran from the store, only to almost stumble onto a patrol car that just happened to drive by. Still rattled by the woman's scream, he fired, hitting the police driver in the arm. His partner quickly drew his own gun, fired at the thief, wounding his shoulder, and soon had the suspect in handcuffs.

The cashier's entire testimony favored the district attorney, who wanted a life sentence for the defendant. But the defense attorney began to question the witness. I was translating the entire drama for the witness. "Madam, what is your true and correct name?"

"Flor Estrella, sir."

"But isn't it true that you are working under the name of Margarita Blanca?"

"Yes, sir."

"So then, are you a liar? Tell us, because you are under oath, what is your true and correct name?"

"Flor Estrella."

"But then, who is Margarita Blanca?"

"A friend let me use her name so I could get a job, because I don't have the legal papers to work in this country."

"So, on top of a liar, you are also an impostor. How can we trust in your testimony, then?"

The heavenly court has only one witness. His name? The "True and Faithful Witness" (Revelation 3:14 WEB). His alias? Jesus Christ. What is his testimony? That we are all thieves, hypocrites, impostors, and even our love, which appears to be so pure, feeds on a large quantity of lust and self-interest. That testimony is given before the Supreme Judge of the universe. Then, what good is his testimony if instead it condemns us? Because when the Judge calls your name, the Faithful Witness answers, "Present." He takes your place. He pleads guilty in your favor. He takes your guilty sentence. And that's not something that's going to take place in the future. It has already happened. "It is finished." On the cross, almost 2,000 years ago, you and I were judged in his body. He gave true and faithful witness that everything written in our heavenly record is true. But for that same reason, he took our place because he wants our life, not our condemnation. He wants for us to live eternally at his side, enthralled at his love. Scripture says, "As I live, says the Lord God, I have no pleasure in the death of the wicked, but rather that the wicked turn from his way and live . . . I have come that they might have life, and have it more abundantly . . . If death ruled because of one person's failure, those who receive the multiplied grace and the gift of righteousness will even more certainly rule in life through the one person Jesus Christ" (Ezekiel 33:11 MEV; John 10:10 NMB; Romans 5:17 CEB). That pleasure, which is nothing but the firm conviction of his will, moved God to give himself up for us in the life of the Son. And God cannot lie. You may think you're denying his will for you today, but God's heart will seek you out even into death! That is why Scripture says, "When he ascended on high, he took captivity captive" (Ephesians 4:8 EHV). Listen, he tells you, "Stronger than death is my love for you" (Song of Songs 8:6 RSV).

41

My Attorney Is Not Helping Me

> "My little children, I'm writing these things to you so that you don't sin. But if you do sin, we have an advocate with the Father, Jesus Christ, the righteous one. He is God's way of dealing with our sins, not only ours but the sins of the whole world" (1 John 2:1-2 CEB).

These words are heard all too frequently from all types of defendants. It's not a baseless complaint. Many times, I've had to translate these words to the court. "He's not doing anything for me. All he does is ask for one more continuance, and nothing happens. I want Your Honor to appoint for me another public defender; this one does not help me. He says he's going to visit me in jail to talk to me about my case, my defenses, my evidence, but they're always lies; he never shows up. He just talks to me a little bit before the court hearing to tell me the same old story, that he's going to come and visit me, and work out a strategy for my defense." These complaints are voiced even after three years since his arrest. It's not just a fickle complaint. There is honest pain, frustration, anguish, loneliness, and helplessness, to name a few.

But the law provides a certain remedy. It's called a Marsden hearing. As soon as the defendant requests a Marsden hearing, the law requires the judge to cease all ongoing proceedings and hear the defendant's complaints. The courtroom is cleared of everyone so that the accused may present his case in confidence before the judge. Only the attorneys, the clerk, the judge, and if needed, the interpreter remain. The defendant must prove to the judge that there is no longer any useful communication with his attorney, and his confidence in his attorney is so broken that he no longer trusts him with his defense. But the judge does not always grant the petition. More often, he dismisses the petition and grants his support to the public defender, which only exasperates the defendant even more. The attorneys try to explain to their defendants that requesting continuances is a strategy in itself. It is a way to wear out the district attorney, grant some kind of clemency, and accept a lesser punishment in exchange for a guilty plea. But the accused only knows the boredom and frustration of marking jail time. Most of the time, they're left in the dark, with the dark thoughts of their crimes.

But before the heavenly tribunal, all is different. We have the most outstanding attorney, who fulfills all promises and obligations. He not only took our case, but also our place as the accused. He pled guilty in our place, received the sentence, and then laid his life down on the cross. That's how he actively and persistently defended our case. That's what it's like to have a real attorney! No wonder Scripture says, "My little children, I'm writing these things to you so that you don't sin. But if you do sin, we have an advocate with the Father, Jesus Christ the righteous one. He is God's way of dealing with our sins, not only ours but the sins of the whole world" (1 John 2:1-2 CEB). When the divine Judge calls your name, it is Jesus, the appointed attorney, who answers. When the divine Judge asks us to render an account of our lives, it is he who offers his perfect life on our behalf. And that we may have the assurance that all is true, the Holy Spirit comes to remind us constantly of our Attorney's work, his finished work. For his defense is over and done; it's been accepted as successful. We are declared righteous in the Beloved. When waves of doubt threaten to overwhelm us, when we feel that we are worth nothing, seeing our many faults and defects, the Spirit whispers to us, "You have an Attorney before the Father; it is Jesus Christ, and your life is hidden away in him." Some defendants choose to be their own attorneys when their public defender does not help them the way they wish. But woe be to us if we choose to be our own attorney before the Father. We have a perfect One; our arguments are imperfect, thus we are worthless attorneys. Our case has already been tried and settled more than favorably in the body of Christ. You don't have to stay in the dark about your future. Your life is "hidden with Christ in God" (Colossians 3:3 CEB). You have a future and a life—more abundantly and forever!

42

They Told Me My Life
Was Unmanageable

> Lord, if you took our sins into account, who could ever be declared innocent? (Psalm 130:3-4).[1]

In less than twenty-four hours, she already had two tickets for drunk driving. The first, when she left a nightclub at 2:00 a.m. The second, when she left another club on the following night at 1:00 a.m. The two cases bounced from desk to desk in the courtroom for almost a year, with various attorneys trying to sort out how to file the complaints. The situation was even more complicated since the lady already had a previous DUI (Driving Under the Influence). The defense attorney argued that the two consecutive cases should be filed as one, so that she would only be pleading to them as a second DUI, and not a third. The district attorney argued that each one should be filed separately, so she would be pleading to a third, and the third DUI was punishable with jail time. Meanwhile the lady had already attended 217 Alcoholic Anonymous meetings in the nine months since the incident, having an equal time of sobriety. With a certain pride she showed the worn-out sheets with the many signatures validating her attendance.

"How did you do it?" asked her attorney. "How did you beat the bottle?"

---

[1] Author's paraphrase, Psalm 103:3-4.

Without hesitation she answered, "It's that the other alcoholics told me my life was unmanageable, out of control, that no one could control my addiction, and that only a Superior Power could rescue me from alcohol."

What a most powerful paradox! The only way to govern and control our life is by admitting that we cannot govern ourselves, and that we are simply way out of control. Totally unmanageable. Our only hope was in admitting that only our Superior Power could bring us sobriety and keep us sober.

In the heavenly court, it is no different. We declare that we are unable to do any work well enough to please God. We admit that the only good work is that of God's Son, Jesus Christ, who lived, died, and rose again on our behalf. That is how we please God; for the only good life with perfect works is that of his Son, Jesus Christ. The rest, no matter how good, are only poor imitations. In order to receive the Judge's approval, our entire life must be wrapped up in the life of Christ. That is how we please him. When we give all the credit to him who willingly climbed on that cross to take our sin upon himself, and thus forgive us, that is when he credits us with his life, and the verdict of "Forgiven" is heard together with the heavenly gavel stroke. When we declare ourselves totally useless to do any good work, that's when we actually begin to do good works. That's the greater paradox! But woe be unto us if we begin to congratulate ourselves for any of those good works. David, the writer of the Psalms, and whose life graph was one of ups and downs exclaimed, Lord, if you took our sins into account, who could ever be declared innocent? (Psalm 130:3-4).[2] We honor the heavenly Judge doing what's good not to obtain his decree of "Forgiven!" but because in his Son, we have already been forgiven. Oh, but what about the signature validating that we went to the program? The Son already signed it with his blood.

---

[2] Author's paraphrase, Psalm 103:3-4.

43

Sane Or Insane?

> For the foolishness of God is wiser than human wisdom, and the weakness of God is stronger than human strength" (1 Corinthians 1:25 NIV).

Jail is like a university for delinquents. The new inmates learn from the old, and if they stick to the rules, they can even get an honorary PhD from the veterans. One of the strategies they learn is to fake insanity. When the defense attorney notices the defendant's faraway look, or a distracted smile, inappropriate laughter or sounds in the courtroom, or is very quiet, motioning to no one in particular, the attorney requests of the judge that the defendant be given a psychiatric evaluation. Criminal proceedings are suspended until the medical report comes back to court. Several weeks may go by. At last, the report arrives. Is the defendant sane or not? Is the defendant able to cooperate with his attorney in his defense? If the psychiatrist's finding is that the defendant is sane, criminal proceedings are reinstated, and he has to face his accusers. If he is deemed insane, he is sent to a mental health psychiatric ward. There the defendant receives training and instruction with the aim of returning him to a sound mind, well enough to aid in the defense of his case back in criminal court.

In some occasions, the report reads differently. The defendant is faking insanity, but he's not really insane. In fact, he's so sane that he knows how to fake and act insane. In a certain matter, the attorney asked me to read the report to the mother of the defendant. The doctor could not have been any clearer: "He is simulating insanity. There's the possibility that the psychiatric medications are causing some side effects that appear as symptoms of insanity, but they are only symptoms. The defendant is in his right mind and is able to aid his attorney in his defense. The recommendation is that he be remanded back to criminal court. The young man is well." The mother, who knew him better, cried out between tears and sighs, "It's because he's been on drugs for so long, but it's true, he's not crazy."

But to the heavenly Judge, it's all the same. We're all either crazy or faking that we are sane. Because it's nothing but insanity for us to be doing the things we do. It's insane how we treat our own planet! It's insane how we consume our resources; it's insane how we treat each other with hate and disdain! And it's a greater insanity to think that we can deceive God with our acting sane! But the worst insanity is to reason that there is no God, no future after death, that we are headed to be nothing but stardust, and that our present and near future is entirely in our hands. If that's how it is, "God deliver us," we cry out in our contradictory agnosticism and atheism. How insane! But, in fact, there is only One sane. He's the one who said such insane things like, "Love your neighbor as yourself; in fact, love and do good to your enemies!" "If you are slapped on the right cheek, turn the left one also." "If you are asked to do a favor, go ahead and do two." If we all did such crazy things, we would create a saner world. But we can't. So the only sane One on planet earth became insane for us so that through his insanity, we might be declared sane. And he did this by doing such a crazy thing as dragging a cross to the top of a hill called Calvary, and then doing such a seemingly insane thing as entering death on the cross for our insanity. "For the message of the cross is foolishness to those who are perishing, but to us who are being saved it is the power of God . . . For the foolishness of God is wiser than human wisdom, and the weakness of God is stronger than human strength" (1 Corinthians 1:18,25 NIV).

44

I Was Always Working,
And Didn't Suspect A Thing!

"Therefore, if anyone is in Christ, the new creation has come: The old has gone, the new is here! ... God made him who had no sin to be sin for us, so that in him we might become the righteousness of God" (2 Corinthians 5:17,21 NIV).

Few things cause me more grief as court interpreter as having to translate to a defendant the words of his attorney: "You are possibly facing a life sentence. The charges are very serious." It was only the arraignment, but the attorney didn't want to wait for reality to sink in later on. They had calendared this matter until the end of the morning session, when all other prisoners were out of the courtroom. That meant this case had to do with a serious sexual felony. And it was so. The defendant was charged with continuous abuse of a minor for over ten years. Just that was enough for a life sentence. It was worse. The alleged victim was his own biological daughter, from the age of five until she was fifteen. The young lady grew up, got married, but was not happy soon or ever after. Her ongoing childhood trauma took her to a marriage therapist. It was there when the whole story unraveled. The counselor was under the legal obligation to report the abuse. Today, at his arraignment, only the defendant's wife was in the audience. Sitting still, tears ran down her cheeks. Between sighs and uncontrollable sobbing, she repeated, "And I was always working and didn't suspect a thing!" It was heartbreaking. There are some readers who will respond with a certain degree of morbid curiosity at this narrative. There are others who will feel an awful chill. If someone feels singled out, that's a good thing. You have no idea of the lifelong damage you are bringing upon the victim, your husband or wife, your other children, grandparents, uncles, aunts, and finally yourself.

I was shaken by the mother's grief. She kept repeating: "How did it happen? Right under my nose. I can't believe it. It's my fault. I was working for them all the time and didn't suspect a thing." But in the heavenly court, anticipating centuries to come, the Judge saw all this pain and said, "I repent from creating the human race. Their thoughts are always toward evil. But I love them. I know what I'll do. My Son and I will enter into an agreement. He will become a substitute for all humanity. He said, put all humanity in my being, then destroy and recreate them in me." And it was so. On the cross, all of sinful humanity was wiped away and recreated perfectly anew in the holy body of the Son, who resurrected from the dead. For all those who wish to find forgiveness from so much evil, and recreation in Christ's resurrected being, it has been done. Receive it by faith; it is a gift of God's grace. When he was born, you were born. When he died, you died. When he resurrected to eternal life, you resurrected. That is your new birth, your happy new birth day. In him, you are a new creature, and forever. "Therefore, if anyone is in Christ, the new creation has come: The old has gone, the new is here! ... God made him who had no sin to be sin for us, so that in him we might become the righteousness of God" (2 Corinthians 5:17,21 NIV). Praise God for the great covenant he made with Christ for our salvation. Your future is not an eternal life sentence, but God's own eternity!

45

They're Crazy For
Thinking I'm Crazy!

"I will destroy the wisdom of the wise; the intelligence of the intelligent I will frustrate" (1 Corinthians 1:19 NIV).

I remember the day as if it were today. I was at the Los Angeles Mental Health Court. The attorney was explaining the upcoming interview. It was for a renewal of a Mental Health Conservatorship. Every year, people who considered mentally incompetent and held in a mental health facility or a psychiatric ward, are brought before the judge. The hearing will review a psychiatrist's exam and the notes from an interview with the assigned attorney. The purpose is to determine if the conservatorship is to be lifted, and the person is deemed competent to return to society.

"We're going to see Pedro. I feel sorry for him, seems like a nice man. They bring him every year to see if the judge can declare him competent. Otherwise, he has to stay in another year. But it's impossible with this man. I've had all kinds of interpreters, and no one can get through to him. No one can understand what he says, nor talk to him in a way that he understands. I imagine he speaks some kind of Spanish dialect," said the attorney.

I had an idea. "Where's the man from?" I asked. She told me the name of the country. "And how long has he been coming for a Conservatorship hearing?" I inquired.

She replied, "Well, with this one, it'll be eight. But it's always the same; we don't understand him, and he doesn't understand us. I think he's truly out of his mind."

I knew the country well. During my childhood, I had some friends from that country and had learned to mimic the accent. "Give me a list of the questions, and his name. I'm going to talk to him. You listen; I'll translate as fast as I can while I talk to him, and you take notes, alright?"

She agreed. We went down the hall, far back to a darkened cell where some eight people were being held. By their appearance, they did not seem well. "Hey Pepe, come'eer," I said cutting off the words and imitating the accent. As soon as he heard his nickname and the accent, the man who'd been sitting on a bench with lowered head, lifted his head and walked over quickly to the cell bars. "Look bud, what's up? Have u heard from mom'n pop?"

"Nope, I've been here all locked up a loooong time, so I don't know not'ing. They won't lemme out; they think I'm off my rocker, but they're the loonie ones, thinking I'm loonie."

It was obvious he was sane. He answered all the questions on my list that I asked, and he answered in that particular heavy sing-song accent, typical to that area. I quickly translated his answers to the astonished attorney, while she took rapid but careful notes. Back in the courtroom, the attorney explained the interview to the judge. He read the notes, and declared him sound and sane. He lifted the conservatorship. The man was released to freedom that same day! An agency from his country received him with open arms.

It is certainly the foolishness of God that he has to speak in our defective languages to communicate his will of love to us. Since the confusion of languages on the Tower of Babel, it's been difficult for us humans to understand each other. Written language with its different signs and nuances of meaning has complicated God's communication with us, and between us humans even more. But God "in these last days he has spoken to us by his Son, whom he appointed heir of all things, and through whom also he made the universe" (Hebrews 1:2). But even so, it was great foolishness for this holy and pure being to communicate by means of a cross, and death on a cross, and there take our sins upon his flesh. This is the great insanity by which we are saved! "For the message of the cross is foolishness to those who are perishing, but to us who are being saved it is the power of God. For it is written:

'I will destroy the wisdom of the wise;

the intelligence of the intelligent I will frustrate' (1 Corinthians 1:19 NIV).

Where is the wise person? Where is the teacher of the law? Where is the philosopher of this age? Has not God made foolish the wisdom of the world? For since in the wisdom of God the world through its wisdom did not know him, God was pleased through the foolishness of what was preached to save those who believe. Jews demand signs and Greeks look for wisdom, but we preach Christ crucified: a stumbling block to Jews and foolishness to Gentiles, but to those whom God has called, both Jews and Greeks, Christ the power of God and the wisdom of God. For the foolishness of God is wiser than human wisdom, and the weakness of God is stronger than human strength." (1 Corinthians 1:18-25 NIV).

No doubt you understood. It was spoken in your accent!

46

I'm Afraid To Love

> "I know that my redeemer lives, and that in the end he will stand on the earth. And after my skin has been destroyed, yet in my flesh I will see God; I myself will see him with my own eyes—I, and not another. How my heart yearns within me! (Job 19:25-27 NIV).

The young mother of three small children spoke to her attorney while I translated. Her husband had accused her of abuse, and charges had been filed against her. She explained that she had been the victim, not he. "He had me by the throat against the wall, and on top of the kitchen table. He was drunk. The children looked on and screamed. I don't know how I did it, but with all my might I lunged forward, and my hands found his face. When he saw that there were cuts on his lips and ear, he said, 'Bingo! Now you're going to jail!' He called the police. When they came, they took pictures of his lips, face, ear; they didn't even ask me what happened. They arrested me and had me locked up for three days. Now the district attorney says I've got to go to anger classes for a year, pay a fine, ten days picking up trash, and twenty hours of community service. Last time when I came for the arraignment, when I got home, he was there on the couch, drinking beer and making fun of me. The house was a mess. The youngest one hadn't been changed all day. It's been nineteen years of abuse; I can't do this. You have no idea what I've been through with that man, and now I'm the one who has to pay. When I look at my life and my kids, I prefer not to have been born at all! He killed everything that was love in my heart. Now, I'm afraid to love even my own children!

Stories like this are repeated a million times a day all over the world and throughout human history. The Scripture tells of Job, victim of Satan himself, the accuser, the first abuser and henchman of humanity, who devastates our peace, and tears our own life away. "Cursed be the day in which I was born," exclaimed Job when he lost his children, all his goods, harassed and bullied by the devil.

His friends came and falsely accused him, continuing the work of Satan. "All this is your fault, Job; you've been doing many evil things in secret. Come, tell us the truth about how wicked you really are."

Satan was able to strip him of everything but his faith. In protest, Job exclaimed, "I know that my redeemer lives, and that in the end he will stand on the earth. And after my skin has been destroyed, yet in my flesh I will see God; I myself will see him with my own eyes—I, and not another. How my heart yearns within me! (Job 19:25-27 NIV).

He traded his desire to not have been born, for faith in him who had given him life, and life eternal. This faith is fixed upon a real historical being: He who hanging from a cross said to you and me, "I am here in your place, I am your death, your resurrection, your life, your faith. I am your beginning and your never-ending redeemed life. I am everything to you and the only real possession you have. And though you may try to let go of me, I will not leave you, because I love you too much."

But some say, "My love is so impure, so toxic, I've been so abused by my own sins that I cannot even love God, let alone my neighbor, and even less, myself!" But God's grace is so abundant that he does not need your love in order to forgive you. He only needs your faith, even though it may be the size of a sub-atomic particle. And even that, I will give to you as you hear this good news. It doesn't matter if you say, "I believe, help my unbelief" (Mark 9:24 ESV). Your love will be made perfect later, when we are eternally with him. For now, his love will cast out your fear (1 John 4:18). In the end, "we love him because he loved us first" (1 John 4:19 NLV).

The Pastor's Son

"Blessed are those whose transgressions are forgiven, whose sins are covered. Blessed is the one whose sin the Lord will never count against them" (Romans 4:7-8 NIVUK).

The twenty-seven-year-old young man was on the witness stand. He had been charged with physical abuse of his three-year-old son. His wife had turned him in. She wanted sole custody of the boy, without visitation from the father. She also alleged that the father drank a lot, and for that reason would lose control when attempting to discipline the child. He had also struck her during their arguments. Now the young man testified that when he was a teenager, he had tasted alcohol a few times, smoked marihuana just once, that sometimes he would argue with his wife due to his long work hours, and the salary was not enough to put enough bread on the table. But thanks to his father's example, who was the pastor of a local church, and his mother's help, he had overcome all those problems.

When the pastor took the stand, the judge had a few questions for him. "Have you ever seen your son strike little Titus?"

"Never," answered the pastor, "my son is a good father."

"Have you ever heard your son raise his voice at his wife?"

"No. But sometimes they leave the TV with too much volume, and my son has to raise his voice just a bit so she can hear him."

"Have you ever seen your son strike your daughter-in-law?"

"No, not blows. It's that she gets in his face yelling at him, and he moves her hands apart."

"Guilty!" was the judge's verdict. He didn't believe the pastor's son, or the pastor. He added a well-directed scolding to the pastor, telling him that he should know better than to cover up his son's mistakes, specially being a pastor. Without looking up at the judge, the pastor took the Bible he had placed on the witness stand, smugly held it under his arm, and ceremoniously walked out of the courtroom.

Before the divine tribunal, there are no cover-ups; no one gives testimony as to the excellence of our character, our almost spotless past, or the ongoing transformation of our lives. Instead, our entire life is totally uncovered and exposed. "There is no one righteous, not even one, there is no one who understands, there is no one who seeks God. All have turned away, together they have become worthless; there is no one who shows kindness, not even one. Their throats are open graves, they deceive with their tongues, the poison of asps is under their lips. Their mouths are full of cursing and bitterness. Their feet are swift to shed blood, ruin and misery are in their paths, and the way of peace they have not known. There is no fear of God before their eyes" (Romans 3:10-18 NIV).

It hurts to hear the truth. Just as it hurt the pastor to listen to his son's deeds and hear his own misdeed be publicized by the judge. But there is another Son, Jesus the Christ. He is righteous, holy, and perfect in love and obedience. The father of all evil could not find anything in him (c.f. John 14:30). Pilate, who judged him on behalf of the pagan world, said after questioning Jesus, "I am innocent of the blood of this righteous man" (Matthew 27:24 MEV). The divine Judge of the universe declared of him, "This is my beloved Son in whom I am well pleased" (Matthew 17:5 KJ21). In our case, our Father does not cover up anything. He does something better. He offers us a Substitute, a perfect Son in our behalf. Our elder brother. He takes our place on the stand. He stands the test. "Not guilty! He's innocent!" Through grace alone and by faith alone, he is ours. He replaces all our violence and hate with his unfailing love. God justifies our lives with the life of his Son. He does not take our works into account, but the finished and complete work of his Son. Such is God's grace. "Blessed are those whose transgressions are forgiven, whose sins are covered.

Blessed is the one whose sin the Lord will never count against them" (Romans 4:7-8 NIVUK).

This grace, in its boundless infinity, is yours. Confess it; receive it. This is your day of grace. You have been forgiven through the gift of the Father in Jesus Christ. Walk with head high, proud and with excited gait.

48

Beyond A Reasonable Doubt

"Workers' salaries aren't credited to them on the basis of an employer's grace but rather on the basis of what they deserve. But faith is credited as righteousness to those who don't work, because they have faith in God who makes the ungodly righteous" (Romans 4:4-5 CEB).

This is the highest standard used in the courts by which a defendant's guilt or innocence may be judged. When it is a trial by jury, all twelve jurors must agree. None of them is permitted a reasonable doubt when they issue their verdict. At the outset of the trial, the judge instructs them on the meaning of "reasonable doubt." "Proof beyond a reasonable doubt is proof that leaves you with an abiding conviction that the charge is true. The evidence need not eliminate all possible doubt because everything in life is open to some possible or imaginary doubt."

Many jurors find this norm difficult to understand. "Am I allowed some doubt?" Yes, but it must be a reasonable doubt; it must adjust to logic and common sense, not just to one juror but to all twelve jurors. The judge's instruction continues: "It is not enough to have a simple little doubt. It must be reasonable. If you have a reasonable doubt regarding the defendant's guilt, you must find him/her not guilty. If you have a reasonable doubt regarding the defendant's innocence, you must find him/her guilty." There must not be any reasonable doubt! The confusion arises because since we began to have use of our reason, we've been arguing over "whose fault it was." We were never too ready to admit fault of our own. It was the other's fault: little brother, sister, friend, classmate, mother, dad—we blamed everyone except ourselves, always justifying our blaming as reasonable!

But in the heavenly court, there is not even the slightest shadow of a doubt of whose fault it is! Did you lose your patience with your child this morning? Guilty. Did you punish your daughter a little too harshly? Guilty. Did you say something to your wife or husband that was even a slight put down? Guilty. Did your eyes take more than a second look at that woman or that guy? Guilty. For all have sinned and are totally stripped of any glory that will declare them guiltless before the throne of God (Romans 3:23).[1] But as that sign comes up on the gigantic heavenly virtual screen, some one else appears under it, and with a resounding cry says, "It is I; I am guilty." Then he went to the cross to present "proof beyond reasonable doubt" of his guilty plea on our behalf. He is our Substitute. He does this out of pure, passionate love that wants us beside him throughout all eternity. What? That the being in whom there is no shadow of doubt of any guilt, would take on the guilt of every human being who has ever breathed oxygen on this planet? What an amazing transformation took place on the cross! The holiest being in the universe was transformed into the guiltiest one! He became the greatest sinner that has ever lived on earth, for all the sin of the world was piled on him. Yours and mine included. Because of him, we are free from all guilt, and from all reasonable doubt about our perdition. Free from all guilt, shame, and condemnation beyond the shadow of a doubt. But what does it cost you? Nothing. What did it cost him? Everything. "But he was pierced for our transgressions, he was crushed for our iniquities; the punishment that brought us peace was on him, and by his wounds we are healed. We all, like sheep, have gone astray, each of us has turned to our own way; and the Lord has laid on him the iniquity of us all" (Isaiah 53:5-6 NIV).

But there must be some cost. At least, it must cost us some faith. But really, faith is priceless since faith is given for "faith comes by hearing, and hearing by the word of God" (Romans 10:17, NKJV). That's faith plus nothing; no work of our own is added to it. Not even

---

[1] Author's paraphrase, Romans 3:23.

faith is regarded as a work. "Now to the one who works, wages are not credited as a gift but as an obligation. However, to the one who does not work but trusts God who justifies the ungodly, their faith is credited as righteousness" (Romans 4:4-5 NIV). True, that's not reasonable. But don't doubt it. That's unreasonable, for that's the logic behind heavenly faith!

49

Love That Kills

> "Stronger than death is my love for you!" (Song of Solomon 8:6 RSV). "Happy are they who are invited to the marriage supper of the Lamb!" "Let us rejoice and give him glory. The day of the wedding day of the Lamb has come" (Revelation 19:9,7 CEB).

The medical examiner was delivering his report to the jury. "The first volley of the shotgun entered through the left axillary region. It was fired at point blank since the pellets had not yet dispersed. Soon after entering the chest cavity, the buckshot dispersed at high speed, causing immediate and fatal trauma due to the puncturing of the lungs, heart, and liver. This first volley was the cause of death. The second shot was also point blank. The pellets ripped the skin from the face, entering the skull through the openings of the eyes, mouth, and nostrils, dispersing throughout the brain. This second shot was also fatal, but it wasn't the cause of death. After the first volley, the victim had his fate sealed." The jury listened in shocked silence, and I was so moved I could hardly translate the medical terminology to the defendant who sat motionless beside me. When the defendant took the witness stand, he testified that after he fired the first volley, the victim attempted to lunge at him with a knife, and that is why he knelt beside the victim and fired the second volley. When the medical examiner took the stand for the interrogatory, he added that after the first volley, the heart and lungs had already suffered fatal trauma and could not have supported the body in a lunging motion against the defendant. The jury found the defendant guilty of murder with malice aforethought. Weeks later, the judge sentenced him to life in prison. The assassin and deceased were first cousins, both under the age of twenty-one. They got into the fight over a girlfriend. She had played them both for fools. But at the end, she lost out on both. One was dead, the other in prison forever. She would also carry the guilt over the death of one, and the chains of the other, for the rest of her life. That was her sentence.

There is a love that kills. It can cost you your life. But seen from another perspective, it was love that took Jesus's life. He loved us first. Defective, fallen, with a deformed image, children of wrath, he loved us unto death, not ours, but his. The unseen medical examiner's report from Jesus's death would tell the whole story. But there was another who claimed he loved us more. It was a false, destructive love. It only sought its own. And its own is to defame, deface, and destroy. But at the cross, it was all decided. There, Jesus took an oath on his love with his blood, and yet, he seemed to have lost it all. The antagonist lover mocked his suffering and death, and sought to bring it to an end with a spear at his side. But Jesus, with a lover's cry, breathed his last: "Stronger than death is my love for you!" (Song of Songs 8:6 RSV). But nothing, not even death could hold love in the tomb. On the third day, he broke the chains of death and the tomb to find his bride, his church, to rescue it and bring it to his side forever. This story has a beautiful ending. It's the only love story that truly ends with "and they lived happily ever after!" "Happy are they who are invited to the marriage supper of the Lamb!" "Let us rejoice and give him glory. The day of the wedding day of the Lamb has come" (Revelation 19:9,7 CEB). This is our future. It is a love that gives life. Close your eyes and look with the eyes of faith. The groom is taking your hand. He's taking you to the banquet-eating table, and the banner over him, and you, and the rest of humanity says, "Love!" (c.f. Song of Songs 2:4).

50

He Left Me All His Dirt

> "Come now, let us reason together," says the Lord. "Though your sins are like scarlet, they shall be as white as snow; though they are red as crimson, they shall be like wool" (Isaiah 1:18-19 ESV).

The young woman was detailing the facts of what happened on that day. "He was such a good-looking guy, so well dressed, he spoke with a great deal of respect, and like a professional speaker's voice. I was about to enter a shopping plaza. With a very urgent tone, he asked me to take him to a luxury car dealer nearby. I knew he was a stranger, and I should not take him. But he insisted that he had left his fancy car at the dealer's and needed to pick it up right away. Further, he couldn't call anyone because he'd left his cell phone in the car! I knew the place was not far. It wouldn't be more than a five-minute drive, and I felt sorry for him because it was so hot on that day. I didn't listen to my self-preservation instincts and finally yielded to his pleas. He didn't want to sit in front with me, which made me feel a little safer; he chose to sit in the back. In five minutes, we got to the dealer's; he thanked me profusely, and even gave me a $50 bill for my troubles. I felt so relieved nothing had happened, and happy for the $50 dollar bill I didn't see the red stoplight and ran right through it. Almost immediately, I saw the patrol car with its red lights behind me, and the loudspeaker telling me to pull over. I pulled over right away, because I knew what I had done. I showed him all my paper work. But the patrol asked me to step out of the car because he wanted to search it.

"Why?" I asked all surprised. "Because of that stuff in the back seat."
When I looked, there was a small marijuana pipe, and several baggies
containing a white powder. "I assure you, I didn't do anything; that
guy left me all his dirt!"

But before the heavenly judgment seat, Jesus never regrets having to take on all our dirt. The "all" includes every single human being
in the history of our planet, "for all have sinned and come short of the
glory of God." It was such a heavy burden, that it took his life. Alone,
he trod the winepress of our sins—on the cross and at the hands of
tormentors who abused and mistreated him as the worst criminal
ever. Why? For carrying our dirt. Scriptures testify: "Surely he took
up our pain and bore our suffering, yet we considered him punished
by God, stricken by him, and afflicted. But he was pierced for our
transgressions, he was crushed for our iniquities; the punishment
that brought us peace was on him, and by his wounds we are healed.
We all, like sheep, have gone astray, each of us has turned to our
own way; and the Lord has laid on him the iniquity of us all" (Isaiah
53:4-6). But we show up before God like the gallant young man of our
story, well dressed and puffed up with our appearance. Others show
up with their great gifts: oratory in prayer, in preaching, intelligence,
cleverness, art, and music. But in reality, we are full of deceit, hypocrisy, addictions, and with false pretenses we take advantage of others,
in order to look our best. Jesus took all our stuff on his body on the
cross, without our request, because we would have rather carried it
ourselves. But he bore our deceptions, as well as our regret over them
because of his unshakable love for us.

"Come now, let us reason together," says the Lord. "Though
your sins are like scarlet, they shall be as white as snow; though they
are red as crimson, they shall be like wool" (Isaiah 1:18-19 ESV).
Remember, there's no dirt of yours he didn't carry. You were made
clean at the cross.

51

Where Do You Keep Your Stash?

> "What no one ever saw or heard, what no one ever thought could happen, is the very thing God prepared for those who love him" (1 Corinthians 2:9 GNT).

Four people were in the attorney's interview room: the minor, the mother, the public defender, and the interpreter. The fourteen-year-old had been charged with transport and traffic of illicit drugs in a school zone. The mother was clearly surprised and upset: "Why, Chuy. Look at the mess I'm in. For being here, they're going to fire me from work."

"Nothing happened, Mom. It's that Coco asked me to put that stuff in my backpack and give it to Mireya. But as I was handing it to her, the security guard pulled it away from me."

The mother spoke up again, "Mr. Attorney, I don't know what to believe from this child anymore. He no longer goes to school. All day long there are kids and some grown ups showing up at the house. He says they're coming to get help with homework, but they're there for just a few minutes, then they leave. He's always buying stereos, the latest computers, cameras for I don't know what. I don't know from where he gets the money; I don't know what to do with him anymore."

"Chuy," says the lawyer, "why don't you tell your mother where you keep your stash?"

"The what?" answers Chuy with an innocent face.

"Madam, this boy has in his house what drug dealers call a stash. It's a hiding place where they keep a stack of money and drugs. It's almost always under some piece of furniture in the room. The dealers show them how to make and hide the hole and remove that dirt, isn't that true, Chuy?"

"I don't know what you're talking about," responds Chuy, looking away.

"Well, if you don't know, I do. Let's go to your house right now, and I'll find it for you, and I'll hand it over to the police."

"No!" shouts the minor. "I've got over five grand there. Let me sell the rest, and I'll give my mom all the money. That's probably as much as my mom makes working in the fields in three months!"

From the heavenly throne, the eternal Judge knows all too well where we keep our "stash." He knows the ones we hid inside and outside. Everyone has some kind of stash nailed to his past and present with all corresponding secrets and hiding places. The divine Judge knows all the lies and alibis we have used to cover up our stash. David, king of Israel (who had his share of stacks) once exclaimed, "Where can I go from your Spirit? Where can I flee from your presence?" (Psalm 139:7 EHV). And God's word admonishes, "What you have said in the dark will be heard in the daylight, and what you have whispered in the ear in the inner rooms will be proclaimed from the roofs" (Luke 12:3 NIV).

But the eternal One also has his own secret. Let's take a peek at what God has revealed. His holy and perfect Son, Jesus Christ, the one being whose essence is nothing but love, is hanging on a cross and spiked to the wood, the nails of our sins. The apostle Paul speaks of the mystery of the cross. ". . .we declare God's wisdom, a mystery that has been hidden and that God destined for our glory before time began" (1 Corinthians 2:7 NIV), for there he displayed his heart of grace and love for his children. "What no one ever saw or heard, what no one ever thought could happen, is the very thing God prepared for those who love him" (1 Corinthians 2:9 GNT). No human being other than Christ saw the cross coming. The prophets saw it from afar, but couldn't imagine its full meaning. That was beyond anyone's imagination. There's a mystery about it that makes it hard to believe. It seems too unreal for the all-powerful, eternal, and holy God to descend to such depths and be buried in "a stash" for the dead. But that was the only way for life to deal with death. To meet it at its burial place and destroy it with its eternity. The stone was blown away, and life led all Chuys out of death into eternity, in freedom to live out their eternal purpose, in God's infinite stash of love and joy!

52

I Didn't Know I Was Divorced

> "For if we have been united with him in a death like his,
> we will certainly also be united with him in a resurrection
> like his . . . Now if we died with Christ, we believe that we
> will also live with him" (Romans 6:5; 8 NIV).

On a certain occasion, a woman asked me to translate some court documents from English into Spanish. "I got these papers in the mail about two weeks ago, but I don't know what they say." In a moment I knew what they were. It was a divorce decree. I translated the writ phrase by phrase. Her eyes got moist and almost fiery red with each paragraph.

"Does that mean then that I am divorced?"

"That is so, madam."

She could not keep back her tears. "I didn't know I was divorced. We separated about a year ago, but I didn't know anything."

I responded hesitantly, "So you didn't receive a notice from family law to respond to the petition?"

She answered slowly, "No, I didn't receive anything," she said once again, breaking into tears. While I waited, I saw that she had another packet of papers in the other hand.

"Madam, and what do you have there?" After a quick review, I realized what had happened. That was the petition of divorce filed by her husband. It had been sent over six months back. She had been summoned to family court to respond to the petition with date, time, and courtroom number. It had everything necessary to respond to the demand in writing. It also warned that response must be given within thirty days, otherwise the petition would be granted by default, that is, automatically.

"No wonder when he saw me at the store, he approached me with another woman, and quite cynically said, 'we thank you for what you didn't do.' Now I understand. And from what you just read, he kept the three houses, the four cars, and all the savings in the bank."

On a certain occasion, there was a man reading a writ sent from the heavenly court. The passage? Isaiah 53. An interpreter approached him and asked, "Do you understand what you're reading?"

The man answered, "How am I to understand unless someone translates it for me?

The translator, better known as Philip, went on to translate the passage (See Acts 8). "This passage says that due to your terrible life before God, there is a divorce petition pending against you in the heavenly court. You are going to lose everything, even your life. But wait, there's more. It also says that Jesus of Nazareth, the Son of God, gave himself over as a lamb, and on the cross he reconciled you to God, so that you would avoid an eternal divorce. Since he was a perfect husband in your place, there will not be any divorce at all!"

The man was the finance minister for Candace, a powerful queen in New Testament times. The officer immediately asked to be married, on the spot, to his heavenly lover. "Look, there's water! Is there anything that would keep me from being baptized into him, right now?"

Paul explains what being married through baptism means. "Or don't you know that all of us who were baptized into Christ Jesus were baptized into his death? We were therefore buried with him through baptism into death in order that, just as Christ was raised from the dead through the glory of the Father, we too may live a new life. For if we have been united with him in a death like his, we will certainly also be united with him in a resurrection like his . . . Now if we died with Christ, we believe that we will also live with him" (Romans 6:3-8 NIV).

Most human marriages end with the death of one of the spouses. But our marriage with Christ begins at the door of his baptism into death, and then he carries us through the threshold of his resurrection and into eternal life. Yes, we've been married through baptism into the life of Christ. A thousand translations will tell you the same thing.

53

The Police Is To Blame

> "Enter not into judgment with your servant, for in your sight no one living is righteous…" "Have mercy on me, a sinner…" "For all those who exalt themselves will be humbled, and those who humble themselves will be exalted" (Psalm 143:2 MEV; Luke 18:14 NIV).

As soon as he entered the courtroom, the man asked me, "Are you the interpreter?"

"Yes, sir. How can I help you?"

He quickly answered, "I want you to tell the judge that the police made a mistake. He wrote down that I was doing seventy mph in a fifty-five mph zone, but the zone was not fifty-five but sixty."

I tried not to smile, for I knew how the judge was going to react, and he did not let down my expectations. After listening with a wry smile to the man's claims regarding the police error, he addressed him. "So, what you're telling me is that it's the policeman's fault."

"That's right on, Your Honor. He made a mistake in writing the ticket. He wrote that I was doing seventy in a fifty-five mph zone when in fact it is a sixty mph zone. The judge could no longer contain his cynical smile. So the police is guilty for writing down the incorrect speed zone."

"That's absolutely right, Your Honor, that's the mistake he made in the ticket."

But the judge continued his questioning. "So, tell me once again, how fast were you going?"

"Well," answered the man, this time not as self-assured, "I was doing seventy."

"And in what speed zone?" pressed the judge.

"In a sixty mph zone, Your Honor," he answered, becoming aware of his self-inflicted wound.

"Well, my friend. You are not guilty because of the policeman's error; in that, you're right." And then, very pointedly, the judge added, "You are guilty because of your own words. You have just admitted you were going ten mph over the speed limit!"

"But Your Honor, what about the policeman's mistake?"

"Sir," answered the judge, about to lose his patience. "The law doesn't make mistakes. Drivers do! Guilty! Pay the fine!"

In the divine courtroom, before God, every attempt at self-justification is only a guilty plea. Psychology may help us understand our behavior, but not to justify ourselves before God. We can't give God the pretext that we were born here or there, nor from this mom or dad, nor whatever our parents did to us when we were growing up. Great king David, when he realized all his sins, mistakes, and defects, in full humility and repentance pled before God: "Enter not into judgment with your servant, for in your sight no one living is righteous…" (Psalm 143:2 MEV). God requires nothing short of perfection in character, love, obedience, and holiness from every single human being that has ever lived—and yes, that includes you and me. But what God requires, God fully and completely provides. In his Son, Jesus the Christ, God gave that perfect human being he requires. Perfect in love, perfect in purity, perfect in faithfulness, integrity, and self-giving in all his works and ways. Scripture describes him like this: "holy, blameless, pure, set apart from sinners, exalted above the heavens . . . the Son, who has been made perfect forever" (Hebrews 7:26,28 NIV). And because of the great divine gift of grace, in that Son there is sufficient righteousness and right living to justify even the least deserving sinner—and by faith alone. ". . .to the one who does not work but trusts God who justifies the ungodly, their faith is credited as righteousness" (Romans 4:7-13 NIV). "Blessed are those whose transgressions are forgiven, whose sins are covered. Blessed is the one whose sin the Lord will never count against them" (Romans 4:7-13). On the other hand, we are free to enter into the divine courtroom like the driver of our story, and blame others for our sins and transgressions, but even as we utter the words, we will be condemning ourselves. But whoever cries out to God, "Have mercy on me, a sinner" goes home justified. "For all those who exalt themselves will be humbled, and those who humble themselves will be exalted" (Luke 18:13-14 NIV).

54

Picture This

> "Here's the man!" "For it is by grace you have been saved, through faith—and this is not from yourselves, it is the gift of God—not by works, so that no one can boast." (John 19:5 ESV; Ephesians 2:8-9 NIV).

It was the day for traffic trials, and a woman was presenting her defense for an infraction. "I sold my car to this guy, but he never registered it in his name. Every time he commits a traffic infraction, I appear as the responsible one for the vehicle. I always get these tickets. But they are not mine; they belong to him. I don't know how to get rid of this burden of guilt for stuff I didn't do."

The judge had little patience for pretexts, so he asked, "So what evidence do you have, lady?"

The woman had come prepared. "Here is my proof; this is not my picture." On some streets, there are cameras installed that very accurately take a picture of the driver and the license plate when someone runs a red light. Then the police send those pictures to the person on the registered vehicle with a summons to appear in traffic court. That's the famous "Candid Camera" fine.

"Show me what you've got," said the judge, still doubtful. He lingered over the printed picture, and the paperwork showing the certificate of sale. His mood changed though, when he joked with the woman, "Are you sure you were not disguised as a man on that day?"

"No, Your Honor, no. Even if I had, I would look like the person on the ticket! That's the picture of the guy who bought my car; I identify him as such—he's the guilty one."

"Very well, then," responded the judge, acquiescing to the evidence. "I'm putting aside the citation. You're not guilty; you don't owe anything. You may leave." With a great triumphant smile, the woman left the courtroom to the applause of the remaining defendants in the courtroom.

Before the all-knowing Judge of the universe, all our transgressions carry our very own name with picture, date of birth, DNA, and yes, God knows what else identifies us before him. But wait! The picture on our summons is that of another. When Pilate presented Jesus of Nazareth before the angry crowd, he shouted: "Behold, the Man!" (John 19:5 NASB). Scripture describes Jesus dressed with a purple tunic and a crown of thorns, the guise worn by those condemned to death. The crown of thorns had been specially crafted for him and symbolized him as King of all the guilty. He took our place in our photo fine. It's his picture assuming our guilt. And on that cross, he appeared before God on our behalf. But on that day, before the frenzied crowd that shouted, "Crucify him!" was not a mere photo, but God in person. "God was reconciling the world to himself in Christ, not counting people's sins against them" (2 Corinthians 5:19 NIV). Our charges were lifted since they were transferred to him. The wrath of God worked its mystery in him against our sins. We were not objects of that wrath. Because he took our place, we are absolved. Before God's presence shrouded in darkness, God accepts our Other's sacrifice, and Good News is announced to us. "You are forgiven, you are set free, no debts to pay. He took care of the photo fines for your sins. What appropriate response could we ever give to such love and grace? "Let your will be done. Be it as you have acted in Christ. I cling to your word of forgiven. I worship in gratitude that fails to find words to express it. Thank you forever, our Father, which art in heaven! "For it is by grace you have been saved, through faith—and this is not from yourselves, it is the gift of God—not by works, so that no one can boast. For we are God's handiwork, created in Christ Jesus to do good works, which God prepared in advance for us to do" (Ephesians 2:8-10 NIV).

55

Espiritus or Spirit?

> "In the last days, God says, I will pour out my Spirit on all people . . . And everyone who calls on the name of the Lord will be saved" (Acts 2:17,21 CEB).

The witness with faltering voice remembered the details of that early morning. "I saw in my rear-view mirror that the lights of an oncoming car were approaching really fast. I didn't know what to do. I expected a sudden impact from behind. At the last instant, the car passed me on the right. But when it changed to the left lane, it just kept going left, out of the road into the median with all the palms trees. I slowed down and saw through the swirling dust how he was swerving, trying to avoid the palm trees. In one of those zigzags, I saw the front passenger side where someone was sitting. The side smashed into the trunk of a palm tree. The car bounced; it lost a wheel and came to a stop on the sand. I ran out to see. The driver was unconscious over the busted airbag, and the passenger leaning back on the seat rest. He was bleeding heavily from the head. There was dust and smoke everywhere. I called 911 from my cell and a few minutes later a patrol car arrived, and a while later, an ambulance."

The driver had survived and was now before a trial by jury to determine his own fate. The medical examiner testified that the passenger's death had been instantaneous, since the impact with the palm tree had broken his skull in several places. The examiner further testified that a blood alcohol test taken on the defendant had shown a blood alcohol percentage four times the allowed limit. It was the driver's second case of driving under the influence. After the first, when he had pled guilty, he had signed a document stating: "From here on, if I drive under the influence of alcohol or any drug, and someone dies as a result, I can and will be accused of murder." The jury found him guilty, and he was sentenced to life in jail.

The well-known psychologist, Carl Jung, said that the name for alcohol in old Latin was "*espiritus*," because its effect took hold of the imbiber like a spirit. Jung said that this "*espiritus*" of alcohol could only be overcome by a "Higher Spirit." This concept was key to the founders of Alcoholic Anonymous. They openly confessed "We came to believe that only a Higher Power than ourselves could restore us to sanity." To this day, AA keeps restoring alcoholics and other addicted persons to their sanity.

There is a day recorded in the history of Christianity when the "Spirit" was poured out over the disciples fifty days after the resurrection of Jesus. In fact, those who were watching remarked that the disciples seemed to be full of "*espiritus*" or drunk, at 9:00 in the morning. "No!" they answered. "But we are filled of God's Spirit who announces repentance and forgiveness of sins on account of the life, death, and resurrection of Jesus of Nazareth." "For the promise is for you and your children and for all who are far off" (Acts 2:39 NIV). With the Spirit of God filling their minds and hearts with that great truth, the life of Christ was theirs. They had life and had it more abundantly, even in the face of death. He was their resurrection and their life! They were drunk with that truth, and that is what motivated all their actions. Jesus Christ is that great Higher Power than replaces our perverse, deficient, and selfish spirit. Yes! That Spirit is for us and for our children!

56

Thank God He's Not Coming Back

> "Come to me all you who are weary and burdened, and I will give you rest" (Matthew 11:28 NIV).

The judge had already issued the restraining order. The accused was forbidden from having any contact at all with his wife. But he insisted that he was no longer violent, that since he had been released from jail, he'd gotten along fine with her; they hadn't had any problems and that he had learned his lesson. Based on this testimony, his attorney requested the judge to modify the order, at least to permit limited contact, which meant not having any violent or offensive contact. But the district attorney protested: "Your Honor, the defendant brandished a knife in the face of his wife! Don't modify the order. He's a dangerous subject; anything could happen to the woman without the order."

The judge affirmed her argument and did not change the order. When the session was over, the defendant continued his claim with his attorney, who spoke to the district attorney. "Fine, then," he said. "Let's call the wife; let's hear what she has to say, and if she agrees, let her request the modification herself."

Two hours later the woman arrived. She spoke to the district attorney as I translated. "What? The judge issued a restraining order? That's great news! I had been begging God for that to happen. Thank God, and thank you all because that man won't come back home to insult me and mistreat me. Things have not changed since he got out of jail. He comes home, acts nice for a few minutes, and then begins to yell and scream, and demand his way. He humiliates me, calls me all kinds of names, and makes fun of me."

By this time she was close to tears. "And on top of that, he doesn't work, won't go out to look for work. I have to support him and his drinking habit. With my work, I have to provide for my three children; he never puts a dime on the table. No, you've taken a huge load off my back. I'm going to finally have some peace. No, no, don't let him come back; leave the order as it is!" As she walked away, I heard her uttering a prayer: "Thank you, God, thank you, God!"

Perhaps you don't have to dig too far into your memory to find someone who would like to issue a restraining order against you. Most of us have provided more than enough evidence. Pious back-stabbing? Kept silent when you should have spoken up? Waited too long to intervene? Cast a vote just thinking about your own promotion? Eventually, someone figures it out and really wishes you would go away and not come back. And then, as much as you regret it, there is no way back to reconciliation. But those are imaginary restraining orders. What about real spiritual ones?

Does God issue restraining orders when we let his name down, when we transgress against others? When it's evident – even to ourselves – that we have damaged someone's reputation, or bettered our own at the cost of someone else looking bad? Would it not be fair for the heavenly Judge to issue such restraining orders and keep us away from others – and from God – for the damage we have caused?

But for God, there are no restraining orders. In fact, it's only the devil himself who at the cross issued a restraining order against God. "Don't let him die for the sins of humanity. Come down from the cross! Why? He wanted to see you condemned, unforgiven, living and dying in your sins and trespasses. But on the cross, Christ set aside that restraining order. He came so close that he took our anger, fury, lust, and unbelief and destroyed it on his own body, and gave us his perfect life through which we live. "Come unto me all those who are burdened and heavy laden, and I will give you rest" "Come to me, all of you who are weary and burdened, and I will give you rest" (Matthew 11:28 CSB).

57

Is There No End To This?

> "Through the disobedience of the one man the many were made sinners" (Romans 5:19 NIV). "For the gift of God is eternal life in Christ Jesus, our Lord" (Romans 6:23 NIV).

The defendant, had it not been for his handcuffs and shackles, could have been the CEO of a major corporation. He was answering to just one charge. The judge announced it with the exact date: "Driving under the influence of alcohol, as a felony." That caught my attention. Usually, a DUI is charged initially as a misdemeanor.

No sooner had the judge concluded when the district attorney added, "Your Honor, he has four more cases for driving under the influence during the last ten years."

One of the clerks chimed in, "Your Honor, on this last one he had a blood alcohol of .33 percent, more than four times the legal limit." Incredible, I thought to myself. The man was not very tall and had a small body build. With so much alcohol in his system, he should have been dead.

Another clerk added, "Your Honor, he has violated the terms of his conditional release, for he violated a restraining order protecting his wife and children."

Another district attorney inserted, "Your Honor, he has five outstanding traffic fines, on those he owes $3,500 dollars."

The probation officer had something else to offer, "Your Honor, he did not comply with the terms of the domestic violence program. Of the fifty-two classes he was to attend, he only went to three."

The third district attorney pitched in, "Your Honor, this last time when he was stopped for the DUI, twenty little baggies of meth were found in the glove compartment." There was silence as it was expected that someone still had something to add. But the defendant himself broke the silence as he whispered loudly to his public defender, "Is there no end to this?"

In the heavenly courtroom, I only face one charge: "Your Honor, this man is a son of Adam!" What? Are we condemned before God because our first father disobeyed? Yes. "Through the disobedience of the one man the many were made sinners" (Romans 5:19 NIV). Satan, the accuser, adds infinitely more charges. They're the many sins of commission and omission that we've collected along our life. But they wouldn't be there without our first father's sin.

But we only use Adam as an excuse to blame God for our condemnation. "What fault of ours is it that the father of our race has sent us all to hell? Is there no end to this?" But the response from the divine Judge surprises us. "For if, by the trespass of the one man, death reigned through that one man, how much more will those who receive God's abundant provision of grace and of the gift of righteousness reign in life through the one man, Jesus Christ! Consequently, just as one trespass resulted in condemnation for all people, so also one righteous act resulted in justification and life for all people" (Romans 5:16-18 NIV). Don't fret over how one man's disobedience caused your condemnation. Instead, rejoice in how you are forgiven. That is through the righteousness, love, holiness, and purity of another, your second Adam, Jesus Christ. You did not deserve your condemnation. Neither do you deserve your justification and salvation. But it is the gift of God in Jesus Christ." It is an alien gift; it comes from another. When we receive it with the open ears of faith, it is fully ours. The mouth of the accuser is shut, and yes, that is the end of it. All other mouths are shut forever. Not even you can accuse yourself! "For the gift of God is eternal life in Christ Jesus, our Lord" (Romans 6:23 NIV). "Her [and your] sins, which are many, have been forgiven." (Luke 7:47 NRSV)

58

I Want To Pay $100 Dollars

"Indeed, it is by grace you have been saved, through faith—and this is not from yourselves, it is the gift of God—not by works, so that no one can boast" (Ephesians 2:8-9 EHV).

A man came into court summoned for not having paid a previous fine of $1,700.00 USD. "Your Honor," he said. "I've got $1,000.00 cash right here to pay today."

The judge answered, "A thousand dollars? And you can pay that today? Go right now to the payment window, and bring me the receipt. Right now, go."

The man did not budge. I motioned to him to exit the courtroom. He whispered to me, "Tell the judge I'll pay him $100 dollars a month until I pay up the other $700."

But the judge had given him an order. I insisted, "Leave the courtroom right now; do what the judge ordered. Go pay. Come back with the receipt. You'll have the surprise of your life." His eyes and hands wanted an explanation, but I directed him to the cashier's window. "Go pay the one grand. Bring back the receipt. You'll understand then."

Soon the man came back with the receipt. I handed it to the judge, who once more called his name. "I see that you obeyed my order. You paid the thousand dollars. I'm going to forgive the rest of the fine. You don't owe anything more. Next person please."

But again, the man did not budge. Accusingly, he looked at me and said, "But you didn't tell the judge that I'm going to pay the other $700 with $100 a month."

I answered him, "Sir, what part of 'Forgiven; you don't owe any-thing' didn't you understand?"

"What?" he said with unbelief.

"You don't owe anything more. The judge forgave the rest. It's over; case closed. Hurry . . . leave the courtroom." I had to take him by the elbow and escort him out of the courtroom.

At the divine judgment seat, the Judge does not look at our receipts for deeds well done, for anything we think we have paid to cover our sins. He only looks at what the Son has done, and divinity is well pleased. The scars on the Son's side, hands, and feet belong to the entire divine Godhead. That's all the proof needed to know that our account is wiped clean, and *no new charges are incurred!* There's no remaining debt! He then asks us, what part of

FORGIVEN

don't you understand? As far as you are concerned, your debt is unforgivable! There's no way you could ever repay it, not even with a life of gratitude, of self-sacrifice, of love to God or others. You cannot begin to repay the debt of thanks, let alone the debt for your sins. The truth God reveals to us is that what we have done with our lives, what our life is and will be has no forgiveness no matter how much money or works you offer. Your only recourse is to hear the word of the gospel that grants faith to your heart. That faith says, "Yes, praised be your name, oh God, my sins are forgiven through Christ's completed work for me. Yes, but. Maybe my 100 dollars will help out, like insurance money, just to make sure God knows how much I appreciate what he did. No. You owe nothing, not even appreciation money. Just let God's grace overwhelm you. And as you do, God will find something for you to do, but just because he loves you. He wants you busy, and out of trouble. For his yoke is easy and his burden is light. "Indeed, it is by grace you have been saved, through faith—and this is not from yourselves, it is the gift of God—not by works, so that no one can boast" (Ephesians 2:8-9 EHV).

59

I Want To See My Children

> "Cast your cares on the Lord and he will sustain you; he will never let the righteous be shaken" (Psalm 55:22 NIV). "And lo, I am with you always, even to the end of the world" (Matthew 28:20 WBT). "For all the promises of God in Him are Yes, and in Him Amen" (2 Corinthians 1:20 NKJV).

The father had pushed, shoved, and physically mistreated his wife in the presence of the children. But now he pleaded with the judge to let him return home. He had been issued a six-month restraining order. But the mother objected, saying it wasn't long enough. She wanted a no contact order with any of the children. The father alleged that it was the first time he had ever done anything like that. He said he was remorseful, and he promised never to do it again. He would go to the anger management classes; he would do whatever it took because he loved his children so very much. With tears in his eyes, he pleaded with the judge to grant him visitation during the weekdays and weekends as well. The judge – who was generally unmovable – accepted. He would get his visits.

The mother broke out in tears as well. "Your Honor, he's never been interested in them. He never even changed one diaper, gave any one of them a bottle. He doesn't know how to be a father. The children are going to suffer." But the judge stuck to his order.

Outside the courtroom, her attorney spoke with her. "Madam, don't worry. I've seen this many times. The dads put on a show before the judge, saying they must see the children they love so much. But afterwards, they may show up to pick up their kids and visit with them once or twice, but that's it. Afterwards, they call and cancel, or don't show up at all. I know it hurts, but give it a month or two, and you'll see."

Indeed, a couple of months later I saw the lady entering the courtroom. With a big smile, she approached me and said, "He only showed up once to see the kids and brought them back early. The next time he didn't even call to say he wasn't coming. I have everything written down in this little book I'm going to show the judge. I came to ask the judge to take away his visits." And it was so. The father lost his visitation rights, and on this occasion, it was he who left the courtroom in tears.

But in the heavenly throne, we have a Father that says, "All my promises are Yes and Amen. The evidence is my Son, Jesus." He not only came to visit us, but to stay with us, here on earth and for eternity. The journey took him through a cross, to take care of the debt we had, and then he dressed us with the robe of his righteousness. Today he tells us, "I am with you always, even to the end of the world" (Matthew 28: 20 NLV).

In ancient times, when a foundation was laid for a building, the inspector would come. After carefully testing every part of the foundation, the quality of the materials, the method by which the stones had been placed, and the concrete poured, according to the plans, he would finally say, "This foundation is 'Amen.'" You may build, live, and raise your families because the foundation is firm. That is the meaning of "Amen," a firm, solid, stable foundation. That is how Jesus Christ is our Amen. In all pain, anguish, confusion, illness, loss, and even in our defects and transgressions, we have a Father who will never leave. Even when he disciplines us, he does it with thoughtful tenderness. His grace breaks our hearts, and that is how we feel the discipline. You may trust that he will be at your side, even before you pray for his presence. That is how he is our Amen. "Cast your cares on the Lord and he will sustain you; he will never let the righteous be shaken" (Psalm 55:22 NIV). Truly we can say Amen to this. He is the only foundation on which we may rest our soul.

60

You Have No Authority Over Me

> "We all have gone astray like sheep. Each of us has turned to his own way, but the Lord has charged all our guilt to him." (Isaiah 53:6 EHV)

On a certain day, a woman came to court for a minor citation. It was alleged she had stolen some pencils and candy bars from a convenience store. When the judge asked her how she pled, guilty or not guilty, she fired right back, "I don't recognize the authority of this court. You, Mr. Judge, have no authority over me. This court is a mockery of the Constitution of this country."

The judge calmly repeated the question three times; and three times she gave him the same answer. Then the judge asked her, "Would you like me to appoint you a public defender?"

To which she answered angrily, "This court has no authority over me. I don't recognize any charges against me."

This dialogue was also repeated three times, and by now the judge was losing his patience. "Madam, if you don't answer my question, you leave me no choice but to remand you right now into custody."

Yes, you guessed it. "You don't have that authority over me." As I watched, the court bailiffs cautiously moved in behind the lady's back. They were checking to see if the cuffs they carried at the waist were in place.

When the judge once again received the same answer, he sentenced, "You are remanded into custody." Quickly a bailiff unclipped her cuffs, put her hands behind her back, and in an instant, she lost her freedom.

As she was being led out of the courtroom into the custody area, she shouted at the top of her lungs, "This court has no authority over me; you have no authority over me!"

But wait. Let's not be too hard on this lady, and some of us may have to wipe a smile off of our face for her irrational, foolish behavior. Before God, all of humanity has taken the same attitude toward its Creator. "You have no authority over me." Scripture says that "We all, like sheep, have gone astray, each of us has turned to our own way" (Isaiah 53:6 EHV). Beginning with our first parents until today, humanity has these distinctive traits: Rebellion against God. It denies God's existence. It goes its own ways. It calls evil good and good evil. We think we have authority over others and ourselves. We are a race of insurrectionists against God, and we call that good. And, what is the greatest rebellion, the greatest sin? Believing that there is no forgiveness for all that perversity and obstinacy. That is why, the same Scripture adds, "but the Lord has charged all our guilt to him" (Isaiah 53:6 EHV). The cross is a microcosm of all humanity against God. At the cross, humanity doubts God's existence: "If he is the Son of God." It mocks his work of forgiveness on our behalf: "He saved others, he could not save himself." It denies guilt and condemnation: "Let him come down from the cross," for he was there taking our place.

On the cross, Jesus put on humanity's mantle—its rebellion, unbelief, blasphemy, and all wickedness of human against human. None of us failed to show up that dark day at the cross. We were all there denying his authority over us, even as we were also present in his soul carrying our sins. At the cross, he became the greatest sinner against God; he became the greatest rebel against God, the sum of all unbelief and mockery against God's person. And as such, he was sentenced to the worst anguish: He was abandoned by God. Yet in his abandonment, he brought us to the Father's very presence. But in the mystery of this inscrutable act of God, his very own soul remained pure. And because he bore our guilt and yet remained whole, we are declared as righteous and true believers, as Christ himself. Such is God's grace that with all encompassing love, he stops all perverse and rebellious mouth. And we say God has no authority over us? Yes, but even so, at the cross we were remanded not into perdition, but into God's eternal love!

61

Did Not Intervene
With Her Own Body

> "'He himself bore our sins' in his body on the cross, so that we might die to sins and live for righteousness; 'by his wounds you have been healed'" (1 Peter 2:24 NIV).

The social worker's report was overwhelming and conclusive. The mother did not intervene with her own body to protect her daughter. When the father shoved the girl against a glass mirror, the broken shards caused serious injuries. The girl's right arm needed twenty stitches in one place. When the father would punish her with a leather belt, leaving thick welts on her legs and buttocks, the mother did not intervene with her own body. When the father grabbed the little boy by the scruff of the neck and shoved him against the wall, causing wounds to the scalp, burn marks to the neck, and cerebral contusion, the mother did not intervene with her own body. The mother did not get any leniency for saying that her husband had threatened to kill her if she tried to stop him. The mother did not intervene with her own body. It didn't help her either when her attorney said the reason for the daughter's punishment was that the fifteen-year-old would run off at night with her twenty-eight-year-old boyfriend. The judge issued a detention order for the children, and a restraining order for both parents. The father for child abuse; the mother for not intervening with her own body. The law is clear. The only way to prove that one of the parents was not complicit in the abuse is to intervene with the parent's own body to protect the child or children. The punishment perpetrated by one of the parents on their children has to be borne by the other parent, even if it costs the parent's life. In this case, both parents lost lifetime paternity rights over their children.

At the divine court, the law is also clear. The sinner must receive the consequences of ignoring the grace of God. But God's grace knows no bounds. It takes those consequences upon the divine self. In the triune mystery, the Son said, "Prepare a body for me, I will intervene with my own body" (Hebrews 10:5 WEB). Scripture says that Jesus Christ himself "He himself bore our sins in his body on the cross, so that we might die to sins and live for righteousness"; 'by his wounds you have been healed'" (1 Peter 2:24 NIV). Christ himself intervened with his own body to receive Satan's bruisings: violence, fury, bitterness, hate, death blows, mockery, sarcasm, and all the more subtle components of every kind of violence. "Surely he took up our pain and bore our suffering, yet we considered him punished by God, stricken by him, and afflicted. But he was pierced for our transgressions, he was crushed for our iniquities; the punishment that brought us peace was on him, and by his wounds we are healed" (Isaiah 53:4-5 NIV).

Notice that the prophet says that, "we considered him punished by God, stricken by him, and afflicted." The prophet is contrasting what the Messiah actually did with what we have thought it means. Unlike the man of our story, the Father did not lash out against his Son. That's what we think happened. But no, the prophet says that, "he was pierced for our transgressions and crushed for our iniquities." Many mock the Gospel saying it is Christianity's passive approval of child abuse and all kinds of violence. They allege that if indeed the Father punished the Son with the violence of the cross, then He is the first abuser. But it was the accuser of our souls who moved humans against their human Substitute before God. The Father brought darkness to cover the suffering of the Son, and to frighten off the perpetrators of grief. For such was the Son's suffering and bearing of our sin that he cried out, "My God, my God, why have you abandoned me?" (Matthew 27:46 NLT). But the Father was there unseen, enveloping him in the darkness. And the Son? He sensed the Father's presence in the darkness, and in the thick mist of the dark, he saw the light of day and was satisfied (Isaiah 53:11). He intervened; it even cost him his life, but he retained paternity rights over us forever.

62

Two Bullets Spared My Life

> "Surely he was taking up our weaknesses, and he was carrying our sufferings. We thought it was because of God that he was stricken, smitten, and afflicted, but it was because of our rebellion that he was pierced. He was crushed for the guilt our sins deserved. The punishment that brought us peace was upon him, and by his wounds we are healed . . . My servant will acquit many, for he carried their sins . . . he lifted up the sin of many and intervened on behalf of the rebels" (Isaiah 53:4-5, 11-12 EHV).

The mother was speaking with her public defender. The tone of her voice was nervous and agitated. "I was fast asleep with my two girls, one three, the other five. Suddenly, I woke up with a strange sensation. In the dim light, all I saw was the barrel of a gun almost touching my forehead. Then I saw my husband's face. Days before I had thrown him out of the house when he came home in a violent, drunken stupor. And now again, I could smell the alcohol in his breath.

He then put the tip of the barrel on my forehead. 'Tell me who you are seeing, and I won't kill you,' he said.

'No one!' I answered. I heard the hammer go down as he pressed the trigger, but the gun misfired. Fear froze me.

'Who are you sleeping with?' he growled.

'No one, I told you.' Once again, I heard the trigger and the hammer. Once again, the gun misfired. I yelled out his name, and the girls woke up. My oldest girl came from the other room and turned on the light. He pointed the gun at her, but before firing, he took out all the bullets and put them back in the drum. Now all the girls were screaming. He put the barrel on my forehead again, but my oldest girl came at him with a baseball bat. She hit him in the back of the neck. At that, he left running out the back door.

"I'm so scared he'll come back. He doesn't know it, but with those two bullets that misfired, he spared my life. Please help me with a restraining order. I don't want him to come back. He wants to kill me."

People's inhumanity against their own kind is always shocking. But it is sinner against sinner, and no one has the high moral ground. God's wrath seems even more unfair because it was voluntarily received by the only innocent person that has ever lived: Jesus the Christ, and on Calvary's cross. It is a historical fact that took place on a real live body. But at the same time, justice was done. That pure, innocent, and holy being housed all of us sinners. There on his body on the cross, all of us were present. None was missing. From the most perverse sinner to the most famous personality, renowned for works of charity, love, and holiness. Jesus had to become sin and sinner for every human being that has ever breathed oxygen on the face of this earth. And when, voluntarily, he took on himself God's wrath; justice was done. Nothing false happened there. His body suffered our pain. "Surely he took up our pain and bore our suffering, yet we considered him punished by God, stricken by him, and afflicted. But he was pierced for our transgressions, he was crushed for our iniquities; the punishment that brought us peace was on him, and by his wounds we are healed . . . My servant will acquit many, for he carried their sins . . .he lifted up the sin of many and intervened on behalf of the rebels" (Isaiah 53:4-5, 11-12 EHV). Scripture warns that every sinner "will also drink from the wine of God's wrath, which has been poured undiluted into the cup of his anger" (Revelation 14:10 EHV). This wrath brings God's punishment with its eternal consequences. But it was another who drank this cup. Another drank your bitter cup to the last drop. This was Jesus acting on your behalf. You and I are forgiven by that sacrifice, and our life was spared because he did not spare his own. He has issued death an eternal stay away order. We are eternally protected!

63

You Won't Be Given
The Usual Sentence

"Then he took the cup, gave thanks, and gave it to them, saying 'this is My blood of the covenant, which is being poured out for many for forgiveness of sins'" (Matthew 26:27-29 ESV).

She was nineteen years old, but already she had been charged with domestic violence against her two-year-old. When she came for her arraignment, the judge granted her a public defender without any cost to her. The attorney already had experience with these cases, so immediately he spoke to the district attorney. "Look," he said, "this mother is practically still a girl herself. She doesn't have any experience as a mom and probably has not had a good role model. She probably smacked the baby around, like she was smacked herself. It won't help anybody to send her to jail. Let's send her to parenting classes where she'll learn how to discipline without violence, and with that we'll help the mother, the two-year-old, and the one on the way, 'cause look, she's pregnant again!"

The district attorney thought it over briefly, and then answered. "Ok, let's give her the chance, but tell her that if she misses just one class, she'll go to jail; her baby will be sent to a foster home, and when the new one is born, Family Services will take the new baby as well. I'll give her three months to complete twelve classes. She has one class per week, for twelve weeks. Let's see how she does."

Now, three months later she came to court with her certificate of attendance for sixteen classes! She had gone beyond the requirement. Her lawyer took the document to the DA, the judge, who then called her case, and added: "Because you've completed the requirements, and completed more that the requirements of your temporary probation, I'm dismissing all charges against you. You won't be given the usual punishment in your type of case. But, let me ask you, what did you learn in the classes?"

The young woman answered without hesitation, "I learned how to be a good mom, and how to love my baby right."

At the divine courtroom, all receive the same sentence without consideration as to person, background, or who fulfilled this or that requirement, or series of steps. The death sentence that sin has cast over us cannot be removed with regrets, promises to do better, or programs to follow, no matter who promotes them. Self-improvement programs or steps to follow—even for what is usually taught as sanctification—are a great help for us to get along with others here and now. But the Judge of the universe regards them as useless, insufficient—yes, dung in order to obtain forgiveness. The divine law requires a perfect life, from the crib to the crypt. But that's where Jesus steps in and says to us, "I already presented that life in your favor, and it's been accepted." When Jesus offered the cup to his disciples, he said, "this is my blood of the covenant, which is being poured out for many for forgiveness of sins" (Matthew 26:28 ESV). It is not about a covenant, an agreement, or a promise that we make with God. All covenants made by humans to live righteously before God have come and will come to failure. The cup is about a covenant he made with the Father. He would take our place, live that righteous life of perfect love, purity, and sanctification—all the while being persecuted and tormented by the devil like no one has ever been. He would also take our sin and suffer everything sin parcels out, pouring out his blood "for the remission – forgiveness – of sins." When he made this covenant, he fulfilled it to the last jot and tittle, saying as he died, "Everything has been accomplished, forgive them for what they have done, and replace their lives with mine!" With that victorious cry, he conquers our selfish hearts and relocates us to his eternal kingdom. If you are sighing right now with wonder and longing, that is the grain of the mustard seed. It is the faith of the gospel finding the soil of the gospel you just heard in your heart. "If you have faith the size of a mustard seed, you will say to this mountain, 'Move from here to there,' and it will move; and nothing will be impossible for you" (Matthew 17:20 NIV). Even if your faith is the size of an atomic particle, your sins will move from the mountain of your heart of stone to Jesus's heart of flesh. The Judge will not even ask you, "What did you learn in the Gospel class?" You will simply bow down and adore for such great love!

64

Nobody Controls Me!

> "Did you not know that I must be about my father's business?... And Jesus grew in wisdom and stature, and in favor with God and man" (Luke 2:49,52 NKJV)

At fourteen, he already had a distant and insolent gaze. We entered the Juvenile Hall interview room, his attorney, mother, and I. The young man claimed he needed an interpreter. As soon as he sat down, he tipped his seat back against the wall. The lawyer spoke first. "Miguel, this is a serious accusation; you could get locked up in Juvi for up to three years!" Miguel was looking intently at some spot on the ceiling. "Do you understand?"

"Yeah," he said emotionless.

"You went into a convenience store with intent to steal, and you walked out with two packs of beer. That buys you up to three years in the slammer for kids." Now the young man was interested in one of his fingernails. The lawyer tried something else. "If the judge were to order a drug test for you right now, would you come out clean or dirty?" The mother gazed at him with profound sadness, pale faced, her lips trembling as if muttering a prayer no one could hear.

"Ah well," said the young man without much interest, yet sarcastic in his answer, "The machine is a snitch, isn't it?"

"Tell me," continued the attorney. "Does marijuana control you, or do you control marijuana?"

"Come on," he blurted. "Nobody controls me."

"Well then," objected his lawyer, "if marijuana doesn't control you, why are you here?"

"It was just two packs of beer, and you ain't seen nothing," bragged the minor. And at that, the mother broke down in tears. Her son kept rocking, tipping back the chair.

No doubt this is the picture of a rebellious, deceived, and self-ish young man, to say nothing of disrespectful. We could say much more about the young man's character, perhaps neglect by the boy's parents, the failure of the school system, lack of involvement by the churches, the government, and point to many other faults. But the words of the young man had a poignant, yet familiar ring: "Nobody controls me!" This has been the cry of every human being since Adam and Eve, each one throughout their generations.

Until we come to the life of the young man Jesus, and Scripture says, "And Jesus grew in wisdom and stature, and in favor with God and man" (Luke 2:52 EHV). Even as a young man, he was already taking our place before God. He was "in favor with God" whereas everyone else in adolescence—or any other stage—has been in "disfavor with God." At twelve, we find him in the temple, deliberating with the theologians and exegetes of his day. He seemed to be asking all the wrong (but right) questions. "Why don't you teach us the true faith? Why are you always pointing out the sins of the people and don't point them to the Lamb of God? Why don't you teach them that sins are forgiven by the sacrifice of the spotless Lamb?" That was his act of rebellion. No one controlled him either. He was only controlled by the passion to live a holy and righteous life before God and in our favor. But he had not said a thing to his parents as to the whereabouts of his adventure. When the religious festivities were over in Jerusalem, he, like many other teenagers, decided to hang around, but on his own terms. He decided to loiter around the temple until Scripture time. Then he went in and began interpreting Scriptures for the unlearned academics. When his parents finally found him, he defended his actions with just one question, "Don't you know that I must be about my father's business?" (Luke 2:49 NKJV). And that business took him from the crib to the cross where he took on our sins that we may confess him as our Substitute. Through his one act of rebellion against sin and evil, he has justified our rebellion through childhood, adolescence, and at every stage of our lives. But because of what he did for us, that last stage is not dying, but eternal life in him!

65

Would You Rather Have A Judge Or A Mediator?

> "I judge no one... I have not come to judge, but to save
> the world... For there is one God and one mediator
> between God and human beings, the man Christ Jesus"
> (John 8:15 NKJV; 12:47 NET; 1 Timothy 2:5 LEB).

In civil, non-criminal matters, there is a way to resolve disagreements between two or more people, no matter how insignificant they seem. Let's say I contracted with my brother's nephew to mow the lawns in my yard. But one day, I find a large, beautiful, flowerpot of sentimental value tipped over, and with a broken piece of ceramic near the bottom. When I inspect it, I find what appears to be a black circular mark on it. It occurs to me that it is about the same size of the wheels on the lawn mower I let him use. I compare the black mark on the pot with the black on the wheels, and it's a match. In my mind, it's clear. He broke the expensive pot.

But when I ask him about it, he says, "I don't know what you're talking about. I don't know how the pot got broken." It seems like a small matter. Do I just replace the planter and shoulder the cost? If he denies breaking it, what recourse do I have? Oh yes—small claims court. I could sue him for the expensive pot. Besides getting the pot paid for, he'd be learning a lesson to be more careful, in less of a hurry when he does his work. I try once more to settle with him, but he's adamant. He's careful; he didn't break the pot. I tell him

I'll have to take him to small claims. He says, "fine"; he's confident he didn't do it.

When I go to file my claim, the clerk asks me if I want the judge to hear the case or do I want a mediator. If I choose the judge, someone will lose, the other will win. If I choose the mediator, she'll help us come to an agreement. Both may win a little and both may lose a little. They sign the agreement. But if they can't settle with the mediator, then the judge decides. So, what's your choice: judge, mediator, or do you just forget it and bear the cost? Or do you decide to mow the lawn yourself?

What about the case we have before the heavenly court? It's no small claims matter. It's a life-or-death case. Do we appeal directly to the Judge? The Judge is obligated to stick to the law. "The soul who sins is the one who will die" (Ezekiel 18:20 EHV). But the Mediator? Scriptures tells us, "For there is one God and one mediator between God and human beings, the man Christ Jesus" (1 Timothy 2:5 LEB). But this is a different type of mediator than the one available in small claims court. The very name implies that the mediator is "small." In God's court, the Mediator is large, infinitely large. His work is radically different from earthly mediators. In civil courts, the mediators strive to get each party to give a little. Little by little, each one yields a few more dollars or whatever compensation they'd like, until both are satisfied (more or less) that they have extracted as much pain from the other as they possibly can. But our heavenly Mediator wraps all parties in himself, dies for them on the cross, invests them with his righteousness, and then presents them before the Father, owing nothing! They have all been reconciled in him, and each of them to the others with the same grace they were reconciled to God. "I judge no one . . . I have not come to judge, but to save the world" (John 8:15 NKJV; 12:47 NET). Then he shows how he is the Mediator: "No one comes to the Father but by me" (John 14:6 RSV).

But there is another way to attempt to come to the Father. That is the wide path, with a door miles wide. That is the way of the law, "For wide is the gate and broad is the road that leads to destruction, and many enter through it" (Matthew 7:13 NIV). Yes, many enter the way of the law, works, deals, arrangements, progress, transformations, giving God little (or much), thinking that God will then give them back a little more, so they can then keep on progressing and walking along the path that leads to . . . perdition! For when anyone approaches the Father through the law, they are asking the Father to judge them without a Mediator. But it's impossible to come to the Father through the law, for the only way is through the Mediator. All other avenues are closed. Coming through Jesus is the narrow gate that leads through the narrow way. For he said, "I am the gate; whoever enters through me will be saved" (John 10:9 NIV). That's it. There's only one choice: The Mediator.

66

Tell Her To Wait
Five Years For Me

> "Place me like a seal over your heart, like a seal on your arm, because love is as strong as death." "For God so loved the world, that He gave His only Son, so that everyone who believes in Him will not perish, but have eternal life" (Song of Songs 8:6 EHV; John 3:16 NET).

"You're not going to believe my story," said the man in custody while waiting for his attorney. "I'm here only because of my girlfriend. She talked me into turning myself in. Inside, the other guys are telling me I was really dumb to listen to her. They say she just wants me inside so she can fool around with others out there. I don't know what to think. What do you think?"

"But what does she say?" I answered.

"That she loves me very much, that she's going to wait for me until I get out."

"And do you trust her?" I added.

But he went on. "Look, another thing is that last week, we got married, right here in the chaplain's office."

"And, whose idea was that?" I responded.

"It was her idea, so I wouldn't have any doubts about her," he said thoughtfully.

"Well, but you still do . . ." I added slowly.

To which he retorted, "Well, five years is a long time" he said ruefully.

After a pause, I added, "Let me understand your doubts. You think she locked you up so she could be free on the outside and run around with other guys. Yet, at the same time she tied the knot with you, a delinquent, punished by society, and when you get out, the only thing you'll have in freedom is lots of problems." He listened carefully transfixed on a spot on the floor. Seeing an opening, I went on. "What kind of woman gets hitched up—in marriage—with a criminal? It seems you've got a one-of-a-kind jewel in Catalina."

Tears began welling up in his eyes. "What you say makes sense, makes me feel better. Tell her that I love her, to please wait for me, tell her, don't forget . . . to wait for me those five years!"

The lawyer told him that he wouldn't get an early release. He'd have to do the whole time. Afterward, I spoke with the young wife outside the courtroom who was there with her mother, grand-mother, aunt, two sisters, and three nieces. Her eyes also welled up with tears when I gave her the message. But it was grandma who broke the silence. "It's that she's already pregnant with Andrés' baby."

It's something to ponder as to whether this young woman was in her right mind to marry a prisoner, and on top of that pregnant with his child. But love has no logic. Or, let's say it has its own logic, understood only by the person in love. The Song of Songs, found in the Scriptures, narrates one of those impossible loves. She, black and despised even by her own family due to the color of her skin, and her poverty. He, the king of a powerful and prestigious nation. The two were madly in love with each other. He sings to her: "You are beautiful, my love; behold, you are beautiful."

She calls back: "You are beautiful, my beloved, truly delightful" (Song of Songs 1:15-16 LEB). There's no letup in their madness. The more people try to pull them apart, the more they fall in love.

At the moment when their love is tested, and the king fears to have lost her, he cries out with the insanity of his love: "Place me like a seal over your heart, like a seal on your arm, because love is as strong as death" (Song of Songs 8:6 EHV). Perhaps some will be surprised that this passionate love story is found in the Bible. But it is the story of God's love even for the most hopeless sinner: "For God so loved the world, that He gave His only Son, so that everyone who believes in Him will not perish, but have eternal life" (John 3:16 NET). He has waited for you all your life, and when you trust in his loving forgiveness, the walls of your prison come tumbling down!

67

They're The Ones
With The Problem!

> "I, I am he who blots out your transgressions for my own
> sake, and I will not remember your sins" (Isaiah 43:25 ESV).

The public defender was trying the case before the jury. His role is to create doubt in the minds of the jurors regarding the evidence that has been presented. "When my client was behind the wheel, he was not yet under the influence of alcohol. He was only in the absorption phase. From the time the alcohol leaves the bottle, passes through the esophagus, gets to the stomach, is absorbed in the small intestine, enters the bloodstream, and finally reaches the brain, that whole process is about an hour. When the police stopped by client, he was not yet above the allowed 0.08 percent limit. It was not until later when he was taken to the police station and the blood alcohol tests were performed, when it appears that the blood alcohol was increasing. But at 2:06 a.m. when he was stopped, he was not above the limit." But the jury didn't buy the story, and sentenced him for drunk driving.

What the jury didn't know was this was the man's second DUI in fewer than three years, which would increase the sentence. That is why the judge, previous to trial, had ordered him to Alcoholics Anonymous. Three meetings a week as a condition of his release. But now, after trial, the judge was about to sentence him. "So, what did you learn in Alcoholics Anonymous?" inquired the judge.

"You know, Your Honor," he answered rather officiously, "they're the ones with the real problem of drinking and driving."

"And you?" retorted the judge, "do you have the problem?"

"It's that I only drove with alcohol just that one time," he answered.

"Sixty days jail time!" sentenced the judge. "Maybe there you'll learn that you also have the problem. You are irresponsible. You knew good and well that you had been drinking when you got behind the wheel and started up the car. And today you have the face to say that it's others' problem and not yours! And I'm taking your license away for three years, and if you drive without a license and drunk, we'll keep you in the slammer for another three years! And if you kill somebody driving drunk, it's life. I'm going to make sure you know you have a problem!"

We should always assume responsibility for our acts. But before God, who can be perfectly responsible? Every human act is open to reproach before the heavenly Judge. That is why even king David pled before God, "And enter not into judgment with your servant, for in thy sight shall no man living be justified" (Psalm 143:2 KJV).

While the drunk driver of our story says, "I don't have a problem," David pleads before God, "Don't bring me into trial, for I've got not just one, but a whole host of problems that will surely condemn me in your eyes." But, wasn't David a man of God? God's servant? In our days, we could be talking about a pastor, priest, a Christian artist of renown, a self-proclaimed prophet, or church leader. Certainly, such a person could enter into judgment before God and be justified! Someone like that surely has the right motivation, self-sacrifice, motivation, loyalty—that must amount to something! *Nada*. King David knew his own heart: "If you judge me, oh God, I would be condemned on the spot! Neither my title, nor the fact that I am your servant, nor anyone's good opinion about me, could serve to justify me. Before your perfect righteousness, love, and purity, I could never be justified. "Against You, You only, I have sinned, and done what is evil in Your sight, so that You are justified when You speak and blameless when You judge" (Psalm 51:4 NASB). Is there hope and forgiveness for the irresponsible? "I, I am he who blots out your transgressions for my own sake, and I will not remember your sins" (Isaiah 43:25 ESV). "For the Son of Man has come to seek and to save that which was lost [the irresponsible]" (Luke 19:10 NKJV). And, what about that man in the temple beating his breast? He said, trembling with fearful self-knowledge, "God, have mercy on me, a sinner" [irresponsible]. What does the record say? "This one went home justified" (Luke 18:14 EHV). Don't look anywhere else. That's talking about you. He who doesn't lie, accuse, or slander, has justified you!

68

The "Armed" Robbery

> "The thief comes only to steal and kill and destroy; I came that they may have life, and have it abundantly" (John 10:10 EHV).

The police were interviewing the victims. The video was blurry, grayish, more like black and white. The time stamp appeared in one corner of the screen, 2:04 a.m. On the other corner, you could see a window open, and two bodies squeezing through the opening. They were masked and hooded, wearing gloves. Another camera angle showed the interior of the car shop. You could see the individuals going from car to car, removing valuables and putting them in backpacks. Then at 2:45 a.m. both men left through the same window, taking care to close it after them. A sergeant explained the incident to the victims. "This is another kind of 'armed' robbery, but without weapons. It's just in the way it was set up. It's all a show. The shop owner pays off a couple of employees to fake the robbery. In the morning, he calls the police and files an insurance claim for thousands of dollars to compensate for his losses. He pawns off the valuables and keeps the insurance money. It's a pretty penny!"

The attorney for one of the victims added, "As soon as we started investigating, the owner filed bankruptcy, his employees have resigned, the shop is shut down, and we can't find anyone to talk to!" We suspect this is big business around town. The robbery looks like the real deal, and so does the claim. But it's all a sham.

It seems as if everyday wickedness morphs into newer shapes and forms to steal away our peace. Violence, wars, and most in the name of God, or some other god. Those are indeed "armed" or setup robberies. They rob God's name of purity, love, and goodness, and substitute it with some show of piety, or some type of religious/political fervor. But it's all a sham. The real deal robs no one but gives everything back. Everything humanity has lost is given back through God's decree of justification. "Justified therefore, by faith we have peace with God through our Lord Jesus the Christ" (Romans 5:1 JUB). In the decree of justification, it is announced that Jesus Christ took on his own body, on the cross, all violence, and all shapes and forms – even the most bizarre–type of human wickedness. There he became the most shameful and guilty criminal. For what purpose? That we may have peace with God trusting in his incredible deed on our behalf. If all were to believe that they were really forgiven and justified in Christ's body, we would truly have peace with God and with each other. That's the abundant life of gratitude. Christ said, "The thief comes only to steal and kill and destroy; I came that they may have life and have it abundantly" (John 10:10 EHV). But what about if we already feel nailed to our own cross for our sins and transgressions, and we can't even show gratitude or work up any good deed to show our repentance? We can only cry out like the thief on the cross, "Lord, remember me when you come into your kingdom!" The answer will still be the same, "I tell you today you will be with me in paradise!" (Luke 23:43 NCV).

69

Elderly Abuse

"For God did not send his son into the world to condemn the world, but that the world through him might be saved." (John 3:17 JUB).

In the interview room, the lawyer spoke with the parents about their son, a seventeen-year-old minor. The parents were agricultural workers. From sun to sun they worked in the fields sowing, weeding, watering, and harvesting. Their skin was tanned and wrinkled by the sun. They were honest workers, disciplined, fully dedicated to making an honest living. But as it happens to many parents in similar circumstances, they neglect their children. Neither do the children value the daily toil their parents strive on their behalf. It was the parents' dream that Mateo would do well in school and benefit from the opportunity they never had. During the interview, the story emerged little by little. The young man had slipped his hands into his mother's purse. He found a $100 dollar bill, for field workers are paid in cash. That represented about two days' work in the unbearable heat. His idea was to take the money to the casino where he hoped to at least double the money, return his mother's $100 dollar bill, and keep some for himself. He had no problem changing his appearance to look much older in order to get in. Once there, he went to the slot machines. Promptly, he lost everything. He didn't know how he was going to repay his mother's $100 dollar bill. Out of the corner of his eye, he saw an elderly woman playing in the next aisle. Next to her was a wheelchair. Resting on the back of the wheelchair there was her purse with the straps hanging toward her lap. It looked easy enough. He'd walk by, snatch the purse and take off running for the first exit. Not giving it further thought, he headed in her direction, calculated the moment for the snatch and yanked! But he didn't realize the woman had wrapped one of the straps around her arm. The sudden tug sent her to the ground banging her forehead on the wheelchair, and then on the floor. She was seventy-five years old. When the paramedics came, she had an open cut on the forehead, blood everywhere, and black and blues over her body. The security cameras had caught all the action. The guards were waiting for him at the door.

Now in court, the lawyer explained to the parents, that as a condition of probation, they would have to pay for the woman's medical costs, ambulance, paramedics, and two days stay at the hospital. The young man got six months locked up in Juvenile Hall for physical abuse against a senior citizen with grave injuries, and attempted robbery. Once free, he'd have to comply with fifty hours of community service. But who got the brunt of his actions? His parents! From where were they going to get the $7,000 dollars for medical bills and damages?

The security cameras also have our pictures, since Adam until now. Our worst transgression? The same as the young man's. We have despised and physically rejected the sacrifice of our heavenly family in giving up the Son for us. "For you know that it was not with perishable things such as silver or gold that you were redeemed from the empty way of life handed down to you from your ancestors, but with the precious blood of Christ, a lamb without blemish or defect" (1 Peter 1:18-19 NIV). "But he was pierced for our transgressions, he was crushed for our iniquities; the punishment that brought us peace was on him, and by his wounds we are healed. We all, like sheep, have gone astray, each of us has turned to our own way; and the Lord has laid on him the iniquity of us all" (Isaiah 53:5-6 NIV). The young man of our story was out in two months, but his parents had to sell a parcel they had bought in their home country with their toil and sweat, to pay for the senior citizen's medical bills. We are free because of the sacrifice of our heavenly family who at the infinite cost of the Son's life, obtained our freedom, and forever!

70

An Attorney Partner In Crime?

"You will again have compassion on us; you will tread our sins underfoot and hurl all our iniquities into the depths of the sea" (Micah 7:19 NIV).

"Today we'll go before the judge. We'll try to convince him that you can go back home to your wife and kids." The lawyer was preparing his client for his appearance. "You've been to parenting classes; you haven't missed any of your group therapies. What's more, in all your drug tests, you came out clean. Here is one, two, three clean tests in the last six months; just this one," said the attorney, showing him the page. "This last one you tested dirty. Last month."

"So, is that going to affect me?" asked the man anxiously.

"No, if you agree, I'm going to take it out of this pile, and put it over here in this folder. I'm going to let the judge see the first pile, and this last one, I'm going to keep. After all, these tests are confidential. If the judge were to see your last test was dirty, you won't go back home to your kids; you'll have to wait another six months."

"So, you think everything is going to be all right?" asked the man, still worried.

"Look sir, my job is to put you in the best light possible before the judge. The other attorney will try to make you look the worst. The judge decides."

"It's your call," said his client, still doubtful. When they came before the judge, nothing was said about the last test, and the man was deemed ready to rejoin his family. Now, was the attorney a partner in crime for hiding the father's dirty test? Perhaps the children would again risk having a drug addict at home. It's a fair concern. But the lawyer's role is to defend his client at all costs, even hiding his mistakes, in order to defend the father's rights. That is human justice. Imperfect and defective, and sometimes, a partner in crime?

But divine justice is perfect and without defect. It has its own name: Jesus Christ. He is defense attorney and represents the weakest, the most vulnerable, and those abused throughout the history of humanity. As defense attorney, he presents us in the best light before God. That light is himself, for he is the light of the world. All his goodness, love, holiness, and purity are shown before God as entirely belonging to you and me. There's no place left for our many sins and defects. There's an Old Testament prophecy that was fulfilled at the cross. "You will again have compassion on us; you will tread our sins underfoot and hurl all our iniquities into the depths of the sea" (Micah 7:19 NIV). Further, God adds, "I, even I, am he who blots out your transgressions, for my own sake, and remembers your sins no more" (Isaiah 43:25 NIV). This was also accomplished with Christ's death. But on the cross our sins were not covered. There was no partner in crime there. We were there totally exposed on the body of Christ. All that we are was displayed in what we did to him, eventually causing his death. Our attorney did not hide our sins, but took them upon himself, then destroyed them with his purity. Thus, he is able to present us clean, without spot or wrinkle before the presence of God. That is why we can exclaim with all confidence: "To him who is able to keep you from stumbling and to present you before his glorious presence without fault and with great joy—to the only God our Savior be glory, majesty, power, and authority, through Jesus Christ our Lord, before all ages, now and forevermore! Amen" (Jude 24-25 NIV).

71

Protected With Legal Status

> "God, who is rich in mercy, made us alive with Christ even when we were dead in transgressions—it is by grace you have been saved" (Ephesians 2:4-5 NIV). "Indeed, it is by grace you have been saved, through faith—and this is not from yourselves, it is the gift of God" (Ephesians 2:8 NIV).

The young man next to me listened intently to my translation of the proceedings. The court appointed attorney explained to the judge the minor's situation. Although not tall for his seventeen years, he stood as if he were a seven-foot Marine. What he lacked in height, he made up with his dignified demeanor. Forehead back, straight, shoulders back, perfectly combed hair, anyone would have been proud to call him "my son." Although he didn't understand English, he understood the importance of the moment. "Your Honor," the attorney began. "This young man was found in the agricultural fields without the company of his parents. He slept under a bridge and ate from the leftovers other workers gave to him. We don't know exactly how long he lived in this condition. Finally, someone called the authorities, and Child Protection Services rescued him. He tells us that his parents forced him to leave his home and travel north with a group of several strangers. He is the oldest of eleven children. When he crossed the border, his group abandoned him. He has walked nearly 100 miles looking for work in this area. With the help of the embassy, we've found his parents, who live in extreme poverty in a small town on the other side of the border. They do not recognize Fermín as their son, and have signed documents waving their parental rights."

I was translating simultaneously, but at this last phrase, the young man whispered, "Seriously? I didn't know?"

The attorney went on. "Thus, I request this court to grant him special immigration status for minors and be turned over to the custody of social services until he's an adult. He will receive English classes and receive a high school education."

Once again, the young man whispered, "I can't believe it!" The judge granted all petitions.

This young man's tragic life was turned around in an instant due to the judge's ruling. What had been a bleak past suddenly became a bright future. What had he done to gain the favor of his guardians? Nothing. How much had he paid for the special immigration status he received, in a country of opportunity? Nothing. When the session was over, he approached the judge and said, "Your Honor, I'm not going to let you down. I'm going to study and work hard to show my thanks for all you've done for me."

"Go ahead, young man, we trust you, and admire your courage."

Basically, this brief encounter describes what it means to be a Christian. We are recipients of unmerited grace. Our sins were forgiven at the cross, destroyed in Christ's own body (not our own); and then we were resurrected to life eternal in the immortal body of Jesus. Two thousand years before our birth, we had already been rescued by the Heavenly Agency for the Rescue of Sinners. He granted us – freely – citizenship in the kingdom of God. "As for you, you were dead in your transgressions and sins, in which you used to live when you followed the ways of this world and of the ruler of the kingdom of the air, the spirit who is now at work in those who are disobedient. All of us also lived among them at one time, gratifying the cravings of our flesh and following its desires and thoughts. Like the rest, we were by nature deserving of wrath. But because of his great love for us, God, who is rich in mercy, made us alive with Christ even when we were dead in transgressions—it is by grace you have been saved. And God raised us up with Christ and seated us with him in the heavenly realms in Christ Jesus, in order that in the coming ages he might show the incomparable riches of his grace, expressed in his kindness to us in Christ Jesus" (Ephesians 2:1 NIV). The Holy Spirit is sent to our hearts so that we may say to the Judge: "Thank you for such grace; I want to live for you and expand your kingdom of grace!"

72

I Love You, My Little Treasure

> "I am writing to you, dear children, because your sins have been forgiven on account of his name" (1 John 2:12 NIV).

It was a total of fifty-seven handwritten letters, with horrible spelling, no periods or commas, but full of love and tenderness. A father had written them to his daughter in jail. She, at nineteen years old, had murdered a young man from an opposing gang. She had shot him at point blank with malice aforethought. That just means a preconceived plan with the intent to kill. The gang had picked her to settle a score with another gang, and at the same time to show herself worthy to enter the gang. But the police investigation led to her, and she was captured and indicted. That was the beginning of a long judicial process. The girl's father had brought her up as a single father. The girl showed no remorse for her crime. She had a cruel, grotesque look, which hid her natural beauty; she spoke with anger, bitterness, and resentment. When she was brought to court for her hearings, the attorney would ask me to translate the letters from her dad. "I'm cending u eity dallars for u to buy fud an coll me wanna here ur vois I lobe u bery much, u r mai little tresur, mai prity girl veri presius hope u get aut soon we trabel n ce ur abuelita." Another letter repeated the same message. In some, the father added "I wrot to u mani taims but no hear noting from u cant beliv u dont hav time to wrait a coupl lains to say how u r but I thinc about u everi moment." There were fifty-seven letters. The topic never changes. To that delinquent daughter, in prison for life, for taking someone's life, his words were always

the same, "I love you, my little treasure, I miss you so very much."
At no time at all does he reproach her for her crime. But why only
fifty-seven letters? Soon after writing the last one, he suffered a fatal
heart attack.

Scripture opens to us the heart of God: "I am writing to you,
dear children, because your sins have been forgiven on account of
his name" (1 John 2:12 NIV). These weren't just words. God himself
in Christ went to the cross. There he took on his own body, all our
sins and iniquity. That's the reason for his birth. He was born from
love, a love finally displayed in all its fullness at the cross when he
cried out, "It is finished!" He had given his entire being bearing our
sin, and thus, annihilating all our wickedness. This is the message of
the collection of books known as the Bible, or the Holy Scriptures.
Sometimes, some parts read as the letters sent by the father of our
story to his wayward daughter. But the message is the same to our
hearts: "I love you, my little treasures." Regardless of how wayward
we may have been – or still are – his letters never cease. They were
punctuated by his death on the cross. However, his resurrection from
the dead makes the Holy Scriptures his living word. The fact that he
now lives for us as our righteousness clears up whatever we don't
understand throughout the Scriptures. In fact, his holy life, sacrifice,
and resurrection are the code by which we may understand all the
Scriptures, no matter how difficult they may seem to understand.
The passion of Christ is the code breaker. Jesus himself said so to
his disciples soon after the resurrection, when he met them in the
Upper Room.

> "Everything written about me in the law of Moses and the prophets
> and the psalms must be fulfilled." Then he opened their minds to
> understand the scriptures, and said to them, "Thus it is written, that
> the Christ should suffer and on the third day rise from the dead, and
> that repentance and forgiveness of sins should be preached in his name
> to all nations, beginning from Jerusalem" (Luke 24:44-48 ESV).

Here's the message again of those sixty-six letters of the Old and
New Testaments: "But God shows his love for us in that while we were
yet sinners Christ died for us. Since, therefore, we are now justified
by his blood, much more shall we be saved by him from the wrath

of God. For if while we were enemies we were reconciled to God by the death of his Son, much more, now that we are reconciled, shall we be saved by his life" (Romans 5:8-10 RSV.) Those letters contain our decree of freedom from death unto eternal life! By faith, grasp the one who sent them. He won`t let go!

73

The Almost Hero Of The Story

> "For Christ also died for sins once for all, the righteous for the unrighteous, that he might bring us to God, being put to death in the flesh but made alive in the spirit" (1 Peter 3:18 RSV).

Three young men and an elderly man, all friends, had been at a birthday party. The elderly man had offered to drive, and so he hadn't had any alcohol. Soon after midnight, they said their goodbyes, got into their car and began their trip back home. But soon a noise from one of the tires and a loss of speed warned the driver that he'd had a flat. The man pulled over, and the young men immediately offered to change the tire. To their surprise, they found the spare was also flat! They were still far from town, the entire desert area was full of sand, there was a lot of wind, and they were out of cell phone range. The speed limit on the highway was seventy, and no one was stopping to give them a hand. While they were lamenting and cursing their luck, a patrol car pulled over. He immediately asked all the men to form a line. He ordered them to obey a few sobriety tests, and when he saw that some were failing to stand on one foot, he asked, "Who was driving?"

Without hesitating, the older man answered, "I was." But the patrol didn't pay him any attention, so he asked again.

At the question, one of the young men approached the agent, and with a drunkard's courage said, "I was. That other guy wasn't driving. I was behind the wheel." This young man's father and the driver were buddies and old friends, so the young man wanted to protect his father's friend. But he didn't remember at that moment those two years before he'd been arrested and sentenced for driving drunk. Sometime later, at the police station, he realized too late that he was being charged with a second Driving Under the Influence. He tried to retract his heroism, insisting that it was the elderly man who'd been driving. Now, a few weeks later he was before the jury at his trial, retracting his initial heroism. But the jury didn't believe him. He was sentenced to sixty days in jail for a second DUI with high alcohol content.

No matter how horrible and unspeakable your sins, Jesus never takes back his word that through his sacrifice, you are forgiven. He took our place knowing the ultimate consequence. Our sins would rupture his soul. Scripture says, "he is not ashamed to call them his brothers and sisters" (Hebrews 2:11 TLV). This is the ultimate heroism. "Greater love has no man than this, than to give his life for his friends—and his enemies." He saw us in the failure of our silent selfishness, in the failures of our best intentions, in the hypocrisy toward our own friends, and said, "Don't take the blame. That's what I'm here for. You are my relative, my own flesh and blood, of my own race." He himself took all our shame and guilt and tasted eternal death on our behalf. "For Christ also died for sins once for all, the righteous for the unrighteous, that he might bring us to God, being put to death in the flesh but made alive in the spirit" (1 Peter 3:18 RSV). He was taken to trial, sentenced, and punished for what we did, not for what he had done. Yet, he didn't retract. He was put to death so that by his resurrection, we too shall live! He will never deny knowing us. His life is our most certain reality on the other side of death. Most people spend their life energy fixing up the flat tires in their lives, or finding strategies to fix them. Don't try that kind of heroism. His life is yours for the receiving. Every mistake you make in life is one more reason to run to Christ for forgiveness. He'll give you the faith you need. And then, he will lead you "in paths of righteousness for his name's sake" (Psalm 23:3 ESV).

74

Fourteen Years Of Work
Wiped Out With Two Beers?

> "For God did not send his Son into the world to condemn the world, but to save the world through him" (John 3:17 EHV).

It was her second case of driving drunk. The attorney told her that instead of showing up for trial and risking a guilty sentence, she could plead guilty to a lesser sentence. The fine: $1,960.00 USD. Community service: twenty days. Driving class for second time offenders: eighteen months (once a week). Other fines and fees: $900.00 USD. Probation: three years. If she didn't accept this reduced sentence (and appeared at trial), she was risking another $1,000.00 USD more in fines and fees, 120 days in jail, and five years' probation. The blood alcohol test was the strongest evidence: .18 percent alcohol content. Mireya thought about accepting the reduced sentence until she asked her attorney about her immigration status. "I'm in the process of obtaining my residency. They've already taken my fingerprints; that means I'll get my residency in three months."

The attorney's answer left her speechless. "If you plead guilty or are found guilty at trial, it is most likely that your residency will be denied, and you also run the risk of deportation."

"What?" she asked in astonishment. "After working and paying my taxes in this country for fourteen years, they're going to wipe all that out for a couple of beers?"

The attorney waited a few moments for that truth to sink in. Then he added another: "That is so. The law is blind to all the good you've done all these years. The law only knows how to condemn you even for the smallest error."

Our situation before the heavenly court is not much different. God's law is not interested in how much you've tried to keep it, or all the good you've done, or your hard effort, and even less your good intentions. With even the slightest thought, everything you've worked for is wiped out. Jesus said that the law even with the slightest feeling of anger toward your neighbor, you had already murdered. With just the slightest desire for another's man or wife, you've already committed adultery in your heart. That's heavy! You may say, "But, really, I'm faithful. I really haven't done anything."

"Seriously?" answers the law. "Let's look at your heart during the past twenty-four hours."

Then what hope do we have? All the hope possible. How? The hope doesn't reside in you or what's inside you. Your hope resides in another; it lives outside of you!

That hope is the life of Jesus of Nazareth. The law recognizes only one life that not only met its standards of love, faithfulness, and purity, but also far exceeded them! Not even with a thought did Jesus sin against his neighbor. His thoughts and intentions were always toward his neighbors' best interests, even that of his enemies. Said Jesus, "the prince of this world comes and has nothing in me" (John 14:30 CEB). He added, "I always do what pleases him [the Father]" (John 8:29 NIV). God offers to replace your life with Jesus's perfect life. Unconditionally. What condition could he ask of us, if our life history is nothing but a record of broken promises? In fact, we are continually under a curse due to our record of broken promises. God's perfect law pronounces it: "Cursed is anyone who does not uphold the words of this law by doing them" (Deuteronomy 27:26 EHV).

But no one upholds the law continually or consistently. That is why Paul says, "Scripture imprisoned all things under sin, so that the promise by faith in Jesus Christ would be given to those who believe . . . so that we might be justified by faith" (Galatians 3:21-24 EHV). "For God did not send his Son into the world to condemn the world, but to save the world through him" (John 3:17 EHV). So, God's alternative offer is this: You give him your life of sin; he gives you Christ's life of perfect and consistent holiness before God. You risk nothing by receiving it, and with it, eternal freedom to live with him!

75

Hound Dog vs. Jalapeño Chips

> "The Lord God made clothing of animal skins for Adam and for his wife and clothed them" . . . " (Genesis 3:21 EHV).

The officer didn't even sound the siren. The car pulled over with just the red and blue lights. "Don't worry," said the agent. "It just caught my attention that you still don't have regular plates."

"The car is new," answered a woman seated on the front passenger seat.

"Then, there's no problem; just show me the provisional sticker that should be on the windshield."

"Oh, my husband took it off; he said it bothered his vision when he drove." In the back seat, there was a girl about twelve years old, anxiously eating some jalapeño chips. There were several other bags of hot pepper chips strewn on the floor and seat next to the girl.

"Excuse me," said the officer. "I'm going to bring a friend of mine to help me check the car." An excited German shepherd jumped from the patrol car, as his handler guided him. "It won't take long," he said. The hound first sniffed around the front seat, then jumped to the back where the girl had been seated, and began to bark at the inside of the door.

"Guess he doesn't like jalapeño chips," joked one of the women, laughing nervously. The agent got on the radio and soon another patrol car drove up. Several agents got out holding special tools. Quickly, they dismantled the inside of the door.

"Well, well, look at that," said one of the agents. "Let's see what's inside this bag." Out came dozens of little baggies with a white powdery substance. He then addressed the women, "And do you think this is jalapeño powder?"

The two women were sentenced to two years in prison for trafficking, and the girl was taken to a foster home. Their husbands were arrested for conspiracy and also sent to prison for similar charges.

Ever since our first parents, we've been trying to cover up our sins. They tried with fig leaves. We try all sorts of ways, even jalapeño chips. We think that somehow, we're going to give God the slip, or convince him that there's nothing wrong with us, that he gave us the nod and has looked the other way. But God has his hound dog: the law. It's also known as the two-edged sword. In an instant, it reaches the depths of our sin and exposes us to his eyes. There's no way to get him off track. There's no good work that will convince him that we have changed or have been transformed. Neither is there such an evil work that will convince God not to forgive us. Doubtless, the law condemns us even before we've been discovered.

But it's even more certain that God uses the hound of the law to lead us to his Son, Jesus Christ, and find forgiveness in him. We plead for forgiveness based on the appearances of the good lives we've developed, which are far from true. Forgiveness for the evil of our life, which however did not put us beyond his forgiving love. Jesus is the only one who had nothing to hide, and thus nothing to pretend. And although there's absolutely no reason to deserve it, he covers us with his perfect life. That grace had already been announced in Eden when God dressed our first parents. They tried to cover up their sin with fig mantles. God was not impressed. They were discovered as fake. But God dressed them up with grace, with the skins of animals. Yes, even there in Eden, God announced Christ's sacrifice; innocent creatures were sacrificed for covering their sin. "The Lord God made clothing of animal skins for Adam and for his wife and clothed them" (Genesis 3:21 EHV). Do you feel the hound is after you? Let it catch you; it will take you to Christ, who will dress you with his robe of righteousness.

76

The Fraying Tie

> "His sweat became like great drops of blood falling to the ground . . . You were rescued from the useless way of life that you learned from your ancestors. But you know that you were not rescued by such things as silver or gold that don't last forever. You were rescued by the precious blood of Christ, that spotless and innocent lamb" (Luke 22:44 EHV; 1 Peter 1:18-20 CEV).

Dress ties have two ends. One is the widest; it looks the best. The other is narrower and hides behind the wider one. But the lawyer was so nervous while he talked with the accused that without realizing it, his thumb and index finger tugged at the tip of the hidden end. He handled the most difficult cases, and this was no exception. Neither was the tugging at the tie; the ends were fraying.

"I've tried finding some law, some previous finding that could help you; but instead, all the laws are against you. No matter how innocently you say you touched that part of the girl's body, she will get on the witness stand and testify that she felt sexually assaulted by you. She will also say that it was neither the first nor the last time it happened. In cases like these, the jury almost always believes the minor's story [more tugging at the fraying end]. Most likely, the jury will convict you. Remember that you have another case pending with another girl. That is why the district attorney will ask at trial that you be locked up for life. Your only choice right now is to plead guilty to a lesser sentence. The DA is offering you fifteen years. I understand that you insist on your innocence. But those girls will take the witness stand, point the finger at you, say you are the one, and tell the jury every detail of what they allege you did to them. The jury will sentence you to life in prison."

He was only twenty-two years old. The lawyer's fraying tie was nothing compared to the young man's fraying nerves. When he stood up in answer to the judge's roll call, his seat was completely wet.

There was another with worse anguish. When Jesus Christ began to feel the weight of our sins in the Garden of Gethsemane, he had no tie, nor a bench to sit on. But such was his agony when feeling the tearing asunder of his being caused by taking on our sins that "His sweat became like great drops of blood falling to the ground" (Luke 22:44 EHV). Hematidrosis: that's the medical name given to this rare condition caused by extreme physical or emotional stress. The capillary blood vessels that feed the sweat glands rupture, causing a reddish tinge on the skin. He was not guilty of my sins and had none of his own. But he took them on as his very own.

The young man of our story felt extreme anxiety when he thought of how the girls that he had abused would look him in the face, point their finger at him, and tell the jury all the abuse he had inflicted on them. But neither he, nor any of us, has the least idea of the desperate anguish to feel totally exposed before the Judge of the Universe. Jesus felt it all and more, but in our place. Even more, he felt the curse of the law, which was totally against him for having taken our sins. It doesn't matter if you believe it or not. Jesus taking on your sins was a reality. The evidence? Hematidrosis. "Great drops of blood falling to the ground." Each one of them had your first and last name, and all your history. But he gathered all of what we are into himself and so redeemed us into and for God. When the Judge calls our name, we are presented without spot or wrinkle, totally blameless before God's sight, in the beauty of his righteousness.

77

Eviction Order
Effective Immediately

"Go out to the highways and hedges and compel people to come in, that my house may be filled" (Luke 14:23 ESV). "So the last will be first, and the first will be last" (Matthew 20:16 NIV). "Come, you who are blessed by my Father, inherit the kingdom prepared for you from the foundation of the world" (Matthew 25:34 NET).

The petition before the court is simply an Unlawful Detainer. The request includes an eviction notice against a renter who has defaulted on the rental contract payments. The property owner has the right to sue the renter before the court and request an immediate eviction if previous notices have failed. The renters offer many excuses. "I lost my job, and I didn't get paid on time; I got sick and can't pay. I had to go on an emergency trip," and many others. Weeks go by. The default becomes routine. The owner does not get the rent; the renter alleges an impossibility to pay, that "perhaps next month." For the owners, the law provides the recourse of forced evictions. It seems cruel. There are cases where little children, elderly, sick, and handicapped are left out in the street. On this occasion, a mentally ill person was living in the house. He had special needs. Due to extreme medical expenses, the family had spent all their savings and could not pay its rent. Five months had gone by. The renters had defaulted all along. The matter was now before the judge. Regardless of the mother's pleas, there was no remedy. "I rule on behalf of the property owner. Lady, you have until the end of the month to leave the premises." She broke down in tears.

The owner insisted, "Your Honor, and with change of lock and key?"

"Yes, with a lock and key order. Take the order to the police station so that they may execute a forced eviction at the end of the month, lock and key to prevent reentry. That's my ruling!"

As we stand before God, it's useless to even look for an analogy. The house of many rooms that he is preparing for us has such a high rental value that it's beyond anyone's means to be able to afford it. Its value is measured by the infinite value of the life of God himself, as evidenced in the life, death, and resurrection of Jesus Christ. Thus, the owner, out of the riches of his grace, has already and eternally paid the rent in advance. Instead of an eviction order, he has already issued an admission order. "Go out to the highways and hedges and compel people to come in, that my house may be filled" (Luke 14:23 ESV). But there are many, who out of unbelief, refuse to accept the admission order. They believe that the news is too good to be true, that there must be some kind of catch and that they eventually will have to pay the rent. Then there are those who think they have the means. The wealth of the sacrifice they make to lead a pious life, the funds they provide for the upkeep of their religious institutions, the observances of days, fasts, rituals, penances, and many other riches. But this currency is not accepted in the kingdom of Heaven. The only currency is the treasure of the life of Jesus Christ, a currency that has already been paid forever. Those who heed the call to come in are the poor, the spiritually disabled, otherwise known as those who hunger and thirst after righteousness, those whose life of sin has them cuffed and shackled, those without a spiritual home. "So that the last will be first, and the first will be last" (Matthew 20:16 NIV). Run for the entrance. He stands at the door and beckons. "Come, you who are blessed by my Father, inherit the kingdom prepared for you from the foundation of the world" (Matthew 25:34 NET). And those who think they can pay the rent? They will eventually run out of money. Then they will still find this sign at the door, "Come, all you who are thirsty, come to the waters; and you who have no money, come, buy and eat! Come, buy wine and milk without money and without cost" (Isaiah 55:1 NIV).

78

Ice Cream For A Touch

> "And Jesus said, "Who touched me? . . .because I know that power has gone out from me." When the woman saw that she did not escape his notice, she came trembling and fell down before Jesus . . . And he said to her, "Daughter, your faith has saved you. Go in peace" (Luke 8:45-47 EHV).

The ice cream man, with his little cart and bells, had stationed himself on the sidewalk near a school. As the students walked home, it was good business. The children would stop and buy popsicles and other cold treats. A few early adolescent girls approached the cart, hearing the tinkling of the bells. "What do you have?" several asked all at once.

"Whatever you like," he answered with a cheerful smile, while opening the freezer door.

"I want this one with mango, and this one with coconut for my friend," said one of the girls.

"That'll be $5.00 dollars each," he said matter of factly.

"Well, weren't they a dollar each yesterday?"

"I ran out of those."

"Oh, but all we have is $2.00 between us," said the girl anxiously.

"Don't worry, girls. Let's make a deal."

"Really? Like what?"

"You let me run my fingers through that beautiful set of hair, and I'll give you the popsicles for free!" he said coyly.

The three girls looked at each other and agreed. Soon they were walking away eating the treats, talking about their good luck. The same scene was repeated the following day, with the same result, except now he included a touch to the face. On the following day, he offered each girl a $20.00 dollar bill, but this time the offer crossed the line. The girls had learned about good touches and bad touches in school, and instead ran home and told their parents. The police came to their home, and with the parents' approval, came up with a plan. On the following day, the girls once again approached the vendor, who after basking them with compliments about their beauty, proposed the same deal as the day before. Moments after, several plainclothes undercover officers surrounded the man. They arrested him for soliciting indecent and lewd acts to three underage girls. The police had installed listening devices on the girls' backpacks and had everything on tape. The sentence? Six years in state prison, and lifetime registration as a sex offender.

Scripture tells us about another kind of touch.

> As he went, the crowds pressed tightly against him. There was a woman who had a flow of blood for twelve years, yet although she had paid physicians all she had to live on, she could not be healed by anyone. She approached Jesus from behind and touched the fringe of his garment. Immediately, her flow of blood stopped. And Jesus said, "Who touched me?" As everyone was denying it, Peter and those with him said, "Master, the crowds are pressing in and crowding you, yet you say, 'Who touched me?'" But Jesus said, "Someone touched me, because I know that power has gone out from me." When the woman saw that she did not escape his notice, she came trembling and fell down before Jesus. In the presence of all the people she told him why she had touched him and how she was healed immediately. And he said to her, "Daughter, your faith has saved you. Go in peace." (Luke 8:42-48 EHV).

Since there was cure for her disease, she'd been told she was a great sinner and suffered as punishment by the hand of God. But in Jesus Christ, she saw nothing but hope, healing, and salvation. She had seen how he sought out the sick and condemned like she, but only to heal and save them. She had also been told that due to her illness, she was impure and could not approach anyone, not even touch them, because she could contaminate them with her disease. She was condemned to a life of shame, guilt, and timidity. But with a courage that did not come from her, she drowned her fear and approached Jesus, but still timidly, from behind. She not only thought, "If I only touch him, I will be healed," but also, "If I touch him, I will be forgiven." In that touch of faith, there was an interchange of blood. Her flow of blood ceased immediately, because she touched him from whom blood flowed to forgive and save her. Blood for blood. Forgiveness for guilt. She was registered in the Eternal Registry of the Saved by grace through faith, and installed in the kingdom of those made whole!

79

We'll Care For Her As
Our Own Daughter!

> "Do not worry about your life, what you will eat or drink,
> or about your body, what you will wear. Is not life more
> than food and the body more than clothes? ... But seek first
> his kingdom and his righteousness, and all these things will
> be given to you as well" (Matthew 6:25,33 NIV).

Some time back, Juvenile Court had taken legal custody of a beautiful seven-year-old orphaned girl. Physical custody had been given to an uncle who accepted to care for his niece on behalf of the court. The girl accepted her new family. Now five years later, she was in full bloom as a beautiful young lady. But slowly the uncle began to notice a certain malformation in the alignment of her teeth. Her chin and cheekbones were being deformed by their uneven growth. When the girl looked in the mirror, she would see the grotesque malformation. Her classmates' mocking giggles behind her back confirmed that others saw the same and added to her embarrassment and sense of inadequacy. She even overheard that they had given her an offensive nickname. She quit smiling so that no one would notice. She'd get home in tears, she lost interest in school, her grades dropped significantly, and she began to absent herself from school. She would look again in the mirror and hate herself. Her uncle brought the matter to the court to request dental coverage for the work needed. After all, the court had legal custody over her care and well-being.

However, the district attorney argued that the court could not afford the expensive surgery and orthodontia needed. "All the kids in our care are now going to want it. If we begin with her, we won't have the budget for the rest."

After hearing other arguments against assuming the financial cost the judge said: "Enough! If this girl is under our care, we have to treat her as our own daughter!" Without any further discussion, he signed the order for her treatment.

And what about us and our special needs? Jesus said,

For this reason I say to you, do not be worried about your life, *as to* what you will eat or what you will drink; nor for your body, *as to* what you will put on. Is life not more than food, and the body more than clothing? Look at the birds of the sky, that they do not sow, nor reap, nor gather *crops* into barns, and *yet* your heavenly Father feeds them. Are you not much more important than they? And which of you by worrying can add a single day to his life's span? And why are you worried about clothing? Notice how the lilies of the field grow; they do not labor nor do they spin *thread for cloth*, yet I say to you that not even Solomon in all his glory clothed himself like one of these. But if God so clothes the grass of the field, which is *alive* today and tomorrow is thrown into the furnace, *will He* not much more *clothe* you? You of little faith! Do not worry then, saying, 'What are we to eat?' or 'What are we to drink?' or 'What are we to wear for clothing?' For the Gentiles eagerly seek all these things; for your heavenly Father knows that you need all these things. But seek first His kingdom and His righteousness, and all these things will be provided to you. So do not worry about tomorrow; for tomorrow will worry about itself. Each day has enough trouble of its own. (Matthew 6:25-34 NASB).

We are all that girl with the disfigured face. But we are under total custody of the divine court. In that tribunal, the Judge of the universe does not hear any arguments against us. We are accused as unworthy, deformed, defective, and incomplete. But the Judge orders that we be treated as his own sons and daughters, because we've been accepted in his Son. Then, "do not worry about your life!" "We are complete, beautified, and made perfect in Christ."

80

Meanwhile, Back At The Ranch

> "How beautiful you are, my darling! How beautiful!" (Song of Songs 1:15 EHV). "I am the rose of Sharon, and the lily of the valleys" (Song of Songs 2:1 KJV). "I have loved you with a love that lasts forever. And so with unfailing love, I have drawn you to myself" (Jeremiah 31:3 CEB).

There's a very popular Mexican folk song called *Allá en el rancho grande* ("Back in the great big ranch"). It's nostalgia for the old homestead where a young man falls in love with a pretty young lady. He makes many promises to her and knows they will someday be together *Allá en el rancho grande.* Well, in this instance, a certain señorita had left her *rancho grande* back home and traveled north to the land of promise. There, while working as a housekeeper in a hotel, she met a young man from a ranch near where she'd grown up. They soon fell in love, got married . . . and lived happily ever after? Three years later, they bought a lot next to her ranch back home, their dream house, where they would grow old together. Five years later, they had built the house, with a fully furnished kitchen, central air, even a large swimming pool. A few years later they bought another house but up north, in their new adopted country. But now, sometime later, they were in family law court, working out a divorce.

"And how are you going to divide your goods?" asked the judge.

The wife answered quickly. "Your Honor, I worked my fingers raw cleaning bathrooms, washing floors, making beds in the hotels so we could pay for the house back at the ranch. That was our dream house. But a year ago, I found in his desk some papers saying that he'd transferred the title to our house to his brother. It's such a pretty house, one that we built with so much effort and love. Today, it has appraised for a great deal. But now, I want this divorce because I also found out he's having an affair! He tells me he won't give me half the value of the house because it already belongs to his brother."

"And you, sir, how do you respond to all that?" asked the judge.

"It's that my brother didn't have a place to live with his family, so I helped him out with the house."

"That's a lie," said the wife. "He already had plans to divorce me; that's why he transferred the title to his brother, so he could keep it."

And then the judge issued this finding: "The house was bought within the timeframe and effort of the marriage. Sir, you had no right transferring the title to your brother without notifying your wife. Find a way to sell that house and give half to your wife. And I'm also going to compensate your wife by granting her the house you bought in this country. You thought you were being clever, but you lost back at the ranch, and you lost here. So ordered!"

Planet earth was intended to be our *Rancho Grande* with our Creator. His dream home for us. But we gave it away for coveting what was not ours. From then on, our greed has been our worse stumbling block. The tenth commandment has that claim on us: "You shall not covet." But our nature is so thoroughly corrupt that we flip the commandment. We think it says: "Go ahead and covet everything, and all you want!" And obey we do. We covet the others' goods, the job of the other, the neighbor's husband, the manager's wife, there's no end to the reach of our imagination. Until God sent his Son to put an end to human coveting. But how? On the cross. There he coveted our punishment and took it upon himself. With his coveting, he paid for our coveting.

With his holy avarice, he destroyed our unholy greed. He coveted for us to be forgiven, so he took our sin upon himself, and in his death provided our pardon. He revealed his coveting for us saying, "How beautiful you are, my darling! How beautiful!" (Song of Songs 1:15 EHV). That is how he coveted us, and through his passion, won our pardon. His coveting for our pardon is the inverse of our greediness for condemnation, and goes beyond it. For all the greed in our human nature, his nature is even greedier for our salvation, and, thus, devours our greed. His greed for our justification is greater than our greed for evil.

But why do we continue coveting? Greed cannot tolerate either mercy or forgiveness. As long as we live, we will covet. But now we have another greed that wins over our greed for the prohibited. Now that by faith, we have grasped unto Christ, we covet what we could not covet before. Now we covet for more and more of his grace, his mercy, forgiveness, purity, wholeness, and integrity in love. You can now covet to love your spouse and children more and more. There's nothing that kills our greed for what is not ours than to covet more and more of what is already ours. That kind of greed is pure and holy. Do you want to see it as a living reality? Look at the cross. There was Jesus of Nazareth coveting your soul. But what about the *Rancho Grande*? It's built, ready and paid for. It won't be taken away from you. Covet it all you want!